MARY LOU RETTON'S

Gateways to

Happiness

MARY LOU RETTON'S

Gateways to Happiness

7 Ways to a More Peaceful, More Prosperous, More Satisfying Life

MARY LOU RETTON

with David Bender

BROADWAY BOOKS
New York

WATERBROOK PRESS
Colorado Springs

MARY LOU RETTON'S GATEWAYS TO HAPPINESS. Copyright © 2000 by MLR Entertainment, Inc., and Momentum Partners, Inc. All rights reserved. Printed in the United States of America. No part of this book may be reproduced or transmitted in any form or by any means, electronic or mechanical, including photocopying, recording, or by any information storage and retrieval system, without written permission from the publisher. For information, address Broadway Books, a division of Random House, Inc., 1540 Broadway, New York, NY 10036.

This book is copublished with WaterBrook Press, 5446 North Academy Boulevard, Suite 200, Colorado Springs, CO 80918, a division of Random House, Inc.

Churches, youth groups, and ministries please call 1-800-603-7051, ext. 232, at WaterBrook Press for volume discounts and special sales information.

Broadway Books titles may be purchased for business or promotional use or for special sales. For information, please write to: Special Markets Department, Random House, Inc., 1540 Broadway, New York, NY 10036.

BROADWAY BOOKS and its logo, a letter B bisected on the diagonal, are trademarks of Broadway Books, a division of Random House, Inc.

Visit our website at www.broadwaybooks.com

WaterBrook and its deer design logo are registered trademarks of WaterBrook Press, a division of Random House, Inc.

A list of permissions for quoted material is on page 241.

Library of Congress Cataloging-in-Publication Data
Retton, Mary Lou, 1968–
Mary Lou Retton's gateways to happiness: 7 ways to a more peaceful, more prosperous, more satisfying life / Mary Lou Retton; with David Bender. — 1st ed.
p.   cm.
1. Success. 2. Happiness. 3. Retton, Mary Lou, 1968– I. Title: Gateways to happiness. II. Bender, David. III. Title.
BJ1611.R48 2000
170'.44—dc21   99-086417

FIRST EDITION

Designed by Pei Koay

Broadway ISBN 0-7679-0439-7
WaterBrook ISBN 1-57856-347-X
00   01   02   03   04   10   9   8   7   6   5   4   3   2   1

To Shannon, Shayla, and McKenna:
Three people in my life who bring me
happiness each and every day. You fulfill
me totally and completely, and it is because
of you that I strive to pass through my own
gateways. I could not love you any more.

Acknowledgments

David Bender—who captured my thoughts, feelings, and passion during our countless meetings, conversations, and editing sessions. You made a perfect writing partner and I cannot thank you enough for your efforts.

Michael Suttle—who from the very start put in countless hours to ensure this project was a success. I could not have done this without your tireless commitment. Thank you so very much.

Trina Storfer—whose hard work, dedication, and attention to detail gave me the peace of mind to know that we would meet our deadlines, stay the course, and make this project possible. Thank you.

Al Lowman—who made me believe that the book would become a reality, and that we would find the best publishing partner anywhere. You were right on from the start.

Susan Miller—who always believed I had this book in me. Thank you for your perseverance.

My parents—for providing the foundation, lessons on life, and raw material that enabled me to find and build my own gateways. Without the family you provided me, none of this would be possible. I love you both.

My warmest thanks to the wonderful people at Broadway Books for their unwavering support of this book: Steve Rubin, Gerry Howard, Robert Allen, Jackie Everly, Catherine Pollock, Debbie Stier, Nancy Clare Morgan, Roberto de Vicq de Cumptich, and Amy Zenn. And special thanks to Bob Asahina for his early confidence in this project.

Thanks also to Laura Barker, Michelle Tenneson, and Rebecca Price of WaterBrook Press for their assistance in bringing Gateways to Christian readers and to Tina Lazenby of Momentum Partners for her tireless efforts in keeping all the information flowing smoothly between everyone involved in this project.

Last, but certainly not least, my deepest appreciation and gratitude go to Ann Campbell, the best editor any author could ever hope to have. Your keen insights, boundless patience, and warm good humor helped bring tremendous shape and substance to this book. Thank you for being my eighth gateway to happiness!

Contents

INTRODUCTION   1

THE FIRST GATEWAY

Family 11

THE SECOND GATEWAY

Faith 41

THE THIRD GATEWAY

Relationships 69

THE FOURTH GATEWAY

Attitude 109

THE FIFTH GATEWAY

Discipline 139

THE SIXTH GATEWAY

Health 169

THE SEVENTH GATEWAY

Laughter 217

MARY LOU RETTON'S

Gateways to

Happiness

Introduction

I get it almost every day. Whether I'm in the store shopping for dinner, when I'm out with my kids in the park, while I'm waiting in line at an airport, or even when I'm in a television studio taping a broadcast, I get it from someone. I call it "The Smile Question." It's not always phrased the same way. Sometimes it's, "Do you always smile like that?" Sometimes it's more indirect like, "You have beautiful teeth. Are they capped?" Or even the very blunt, "Are you for real?" However they ask it, it's all really the same question: "Why are you always smiling? Why do you always *seem* so happy?"

And I always answer truthfully: "Because I really *am* happy." Oh sure, I have my good days and my bad days like everyone else. The store line is too long, the kids are cranky, I've missed my plane, or the taping isn't going well. Those things aren't fun, but none of them has anything to do with the question of whether I'm truly, fundamentally happy. Because that big smile people see on the outside comes from a place deep within me that isn't affected by any of those day-to-day matters. True joy and contentment are within reach for all of us, no matter how bad our circumstances may seem. If it rains every day of the tropical vacation we've planned for so long, if a loved one develops a serious illness, or if our investments take an unforeseen dive, we can still grab hold of the happiness that is ours for the taking.

You just have to know how.

That's what this book is all about: How to discover true happiness and live out that happiness in every area of life, any day and every day. You may not believe that such a life is possible, but let me assure you, it is. You just need to believe in it and actively pursue it. If you think your marriage or relationship isn't working, if the shape of your body seems unattractive to you, if your career is more draining than satisfying, if you're convinced that you're stuck in a bad place you'd rather not be, then I'm sorry to tell you this: You're right. The good news is that these problems are only true because *you've let them be true*. And the only way you can change any of them is by working on them from the inside out.

Our success and happiness depend on the decisions we make every day. The external conditions that we face in our daily lives—the crowded bus, the screaming baby next to us in the supermarket checkout line—are just that: external conditions. They are the outer trappings of our lives, and as such, they are often beyond our control. But we *always* have control over what we feel inside and how we cope with challenges and difficult circumstances. The first step in finding happiness is to stop relying on the outside world to get us there—we need to look deep into our own hearts and souls to find the peace and satisfaction that brings a shining smile to our face. A divorce won't solve your relationship problems, larger clothes won't change how you feel about your body, and changing jobs doesn't mean you'll like the next one any better. But if you can discover how to be happy despite all these things, everything gets turned around. If *you're* happy, the world around you becomes a happier place. People respond to you more positively. And all of a sudden the problems you thought you could *never* solve begin to get fixed. As Helen Keller said, "It is not what we see and touch or that which others do for us which makes us happy; it is that which we think and feel and do, first for the other person and then for ourselves."

The best part of all of it is that you can start today. This very minute. Because happiness is not just around the corner, it's even closer—it's within your reach right now.

ON AUGUST 3, 1984, I stopped being just Mary Lou Retton from Fairmont, West Virginia, and discovered that overnight I'd become "America's Sweetheart." The nickname used to make me wince a little every time I heard it, since in my nine years of intensive gymnastics training, I'd had no time to go on dates, much less be anyone's sweetheart. Suddenly I was getting marriage proposals in the mail! But more important, at the age of sixteen, I was about to grow up in front of the whole world. My once private life was now very public. It was exciting, but there were plenty of times when I wished I could go back to being a regular teenager, hanging out with friends and worrying about my date for the prom instead of meeting with top-level advertising executives about product endorsements. Without the support of my parents, my sister, my brothers, and Shannon Kelley (who quickly became *my* sweetheart and the love of my life), and without the strength I received from my faith in the Lord, I never would have made it through this difficult period. They helped me to understand that this overwhelming transformation in my life was not something to run away from, but rather to embrace. I came to realize that it was just one part of the larger journey I was on—what Dr. Billy Graham calls our "journey toward happiness."

Since the Olympics, I've undergone a number of life-changing experiences—my marriage, the births of my children, a major career change. Throughout our lives we'll all experience many such transformative events—some positive, some negative. But the lesson I learned after winning the gold medal applies equally to all of them: No matter what happens, remember to stay focused on your larger journey and its destination—Happiness.

Many people think my journey ended with my winning a gold medal in gymnastics during the 1984 Olympics. Certainly, I'll always be identified with that moment in time and I'm as proud of it today as I was then. Perhaps even more so now, because over the intervening years I've seen the actual proof of how my personal achievement actually inspired and motivated thousands of other people—particularly women and girls, but a lot of men as well—to pursue their own dreams.

Here's the funny part: Even with all my preparation and training for success in the Olympics, I was never aware that I was also preparing for something else. Something which would last me for the rest of my life, long after I was able to mount a balance beam or stick a perfect landing. Now, as a woman not a girl, as a wife and mother who also maintains a demanding professional life, I realize that all of that perseverance, determination, and hard work were training me for something much more important than any single athletic competition. I was training for happiness.

I've always believed in taking risks. In 1992, *USA Today* asked me to write a daily column from the Summer Olympic Games in Barcelona. The columns would offer a running commentary on the competitions and share the personal stories of the athletes, all flavored with the insights of someone who had stood in front of the crowds years before and performed on behalf of their country. Many of my friends and advisers saw it as a mistake for me and they gave me a lot of good reasons why I shouldn't do it. *"You could embarrass yourself." "You'll be on a daily deadline with the kind of pressure you're not used to." "You don't need to do this to be successful."*

What they said was certainly persuasive. I'm not a journalist and although I'd been doing network sports commentary and giving motivational speeches around the country for almost a decade, I hadn't done any regular writing since my school days. If I agreed, it meant taking the risk of putting my name and reputation on the line every day in a brand-new medium where there was a chance that I could fail in a very public way. It didn't take me long to decide.

If I've learned anything from my gymnastics career or from the motivational speeches I give, it's this: You can always *avoid* taking risks and meeting new challenges. Avoiding them is, without question, the easy way out. But it's only by taking those risks and meeting those challenges *head-on* that you can ever break out of your personal comfort zone and reach new levels of happiness and personal satisfaction. In sports terminology, it's called raising the level of your game. In life, it's called *growing*.

Even though it may seem counterintuitive, a comfort zone is a dangerous place to be. Your comfort zone is, naturally, the place where you are comfortable. It's an easy place to reside because you know everything about it and it doesn't offer much in the way of challenges. It's kind of like that cushy recliner and big-screen television you have in your recreation room at home—it's enjoyable, safe, and you can sit there for hours and be entertained with minimal effort. But as we all know, being a couch potato isn't healthy, and it certainly gets boring after a while. Most important, if we stay on that couch for too long, *we* become boring as individuals. Keeping life interesting requires that we get up off the couch and venture out into the world. We may not always like what we find, but it's the unforeseen interactions, adventures, and lessons that shape our personalities and make us valuable friends, spouses, and parents. Remember what I said earlier about life being a journey? Well, you can't start your journey toward happiness if you're determined never to leave the house.

In real life, our comfort zone is rarely an actual place. Usually it pertains to a situation that, while it may have initially brought us great happiness and satisfaction, doesn't offer much in the way of rewards or personal growth anymore. If you take a moment to reflect on your own life experiences, or those of your friends, you'll know what I mean. We've all stayed in jobs that no longer provide us with new challenges and opportunities, simply because we are overwhelmed by the thought of conducting an extensive job search. Or in a romantic relationship that has lost its spark because we are afraid of being alone. Comfort zones are comfortable, no doubt about it—but they are rarely the best that life has to offer. Perhaps the most important step in your journey toward happiness is learning to recognize when you are idling in your comfort zone—and making the choice to stride boldly forward out into the world where happiness can actually find you.

When *USA Today* offered me the job writing a daily column, I knew that this was a terrific opportunity to step outside my familiar world and accept a challenge that would allow me not only to try something new but to give something back to the Olympics and the fans who had played such a defining role in my own life. Was I scared? Of course. In the back of my mind all the doubts and concerns expressed by my friends and advisers scampered around like a bunch of circus clowns. But I know from experience that fear is often God's way of showing us which mountain we should climb next. So I summoned up my courage, accepted the job, and hopped on a plane to Barcelona.

As anyone who writes for a living knows, the pace of journalism is absolutely frantic, and once I got to Barcelona I faced a whole new set of challenges: daily deadlines, scrambling for ideas and interviews, and being apart from my husband.

But I toughed it out, and to my delight, my columns were extremely well received. Enough so that USA Today invited me back four years later to cover the Summer Games in Atlanta. In the end, writing those columns has become one of my most treasured experiences. I've talked with people and learned things that I never would have if I had just stuck to giving motivational speeches. I interviewed everyone from Hillary Rodham Clinton to Michael Jordan. I did columns about the drug testing of the athletes and the tragic Olympic bombing. I was there when Kerri Strug displayed her remarkable moment of courage in the team finals that electrified the world. I was able to bring the excitement of the Olympics to readers all over the globe and assess the happenings through the perspective of my own experience. Best of all, I had a fantastic time doing it.

I HAD THOUGHT about writing a book for some time, but I don't think that I would have had the courage to do it if I hadn't given the job with USA Today a try. It's one thing to talk about your experiences in a speech or in an interview—it's another thing altogether to write about them, and to present them in a way that is meaningful to others. I originally began giving motivational speeches because I believed that people could benefit from the many lessons I've learned over the years—not just through winning the gold medal, but through my experiences as an athlete, career woman, mother, and wife. To tell you the truth, I probably couldn't have written this book before now, because I'm still coming to fully understand the nature—and significance—of these experiences. Learning is an ongoing process, and all of us, as human beings, are works in progress.

But the one thing that I have figured out is what makes *me* happy. As I said earlier, people frequently ask me how I always manage to stay so positive. Maybe it's because of my smile, but they always seem to think I have the answers. And I'm pleased to say that I do—at least the answers that work for me. Naturally, happiness is different for everyone. If you're a musician, you may find happiness spending hours alone in your apartment with your guitar, practicing and composing songs. If you're a parent, you might find happiness playing in the sand with your children at the beach. But even with so many personal variations, I believe that our happiness depends on how we respond to certain basic opportunities, or gateways, that God has opened to each and every one of us.

In this book, I've identified the seven major gateways that I've crossed through during my personal and professional life that have greatly contributed to my overall sense of accomplishment and well-being. A gateway isn't a literal doorway—rather it symbolizes a collection of lessons and experiences that, once understood and embraced, will take us one step farther down the road to true happiness. On the journey of life, these seven gateways are the signposts that will guide you and keep you moving forward. And just as it was once my dream to be the best gymnast in the world, it's now my dream—and my goal—to inspire you to walk through these gateways for yourself and win the biggest prize of all: an exciting, rewarding, and extremely fulfilling life.

Some of these gateways, like Family, are open to us from childhood. Others, like Attitude or Health, we must choose to enter ourselves. When I became a mother, it finally dawned on me that all the things I instinctively know how to do now—work closely with others, cultivate authentic relationships, handle pressure with laughter and humor, speak my mind honestly and directly, and persevere through tough times and challenges—were all gateways that I'd first discovered as a child, and that were reinforced later, during my training for the Olympics and my career. But while as children we all have people to coach us and point us in the right direction—our parents, teachers, mentors, or in my case, an actual coach, Bela Karolyi—as adults we must learn to coach ourselves. This is often the hardest part of growing up.

In this book, I want to be your coach. I want to share with you the lessons I've learned, and help you get started on your own exhilarating journey toward happiness. By showing you the ways in which I've been able to walk through these gateways for myself, and providing you with tools you can use in your own life, I hope to guide you to a place where you can be your own coach and find happiness on a daily basis, without any help from me.

Remember, being happy isn't something that simply comes to us without effort. It's an ongoing challenge that we all face every day, especially in an unpredictable world where our strength and faith are constantly being tested. You'll find that even after you've passed through each of the gateways, you'll need to go back and revisit them from time to time. It is my greatest hope that this book will be a cherished guide that you will turn to again and again. If you do, I know that when I see you in the store, at the gym, or in an airport, or—even better—when you see *yourself* in the mirror, that big smile will belong to you.

Family

*No matter what you've done for yourself
or for humanity, if you can't look back
on having given love and attention to
your own family, what have you really
accomplished?*

LEE IACOCCA

Our journey toward happiness begins the moment we are born, when we enter the world, innocent and wide-eyed, and hungry for what life has to teach us. You may wonder, what does a child, or newborn, know about what it takes to be happy? But let me assure you: Very young children intuitively reach for the first gateway each time they hold out their arms to be loved, nestle into their mother's lap, or look up, searching, into the faces of the brothers and sisters gathered around their crib or playpen. They instinctively know that the warmth, comfort, love, and security they crave can all be found with the members of their family.

Family is the first gateway to happiness, and it's the only one of the seven gateways that's open to us right from birth, from that magic moment when we first open our eyes as infants and see two (or more) much bigger eyes looking back at us—eyes that are filled with hope and joy, with tenderness and love. These eyes tell us instantly that we are not alone and begin to form the boundaries of our fragile world. Families give our lives a history and context; we are an inextricable part of a larger unit complete with its own unique challenges and gifts. Families play an incredibly important role in shaping the person we ultimately become—and, if we let them, they can be an invaluable source of support and stability in our often unpredictable lives.

It is frequently said that the strongest, most unshakable bond between humans is the love of a mother for her child. And it is this special closeness that forms the heart of the family unit. The love our parents have for us usually creates one of the most enduring and rewarding relationships we'll ever have. In the best of circumstances, the unconditional love we receive from our parents and, if we have them, from our siblings, provides us with a kind of acceptance and security we can always rely on to help us over life's stumbling blocks and bring us happiness throughout our lives.

This certainly doesn't mean that your family has to be the picture of storybook perfection in order to bring something valuable to your life. In fact, very few families are perfect. They are comprised of human beings, after all, and no matter how good our intentions, there are always going to be bumps along the path. You may be an only child, or have a strained relationship with your parents, or feel infinitely closer to your group of friends than you actually do to your family members. But no matter what your situation, the gateway of family is always open to you, and you can share in the tremendous joy it brings if you are willing to make the effort.

The bond we share with our family members stands out among the rest of our relationships, because, often, our families know us better than just about anyone else. Our parents have watched us grow and change; they know how we respond when we are hurt or scared; they know and accept our strengths and weaknesses. Our siblings share some of our most cherished memories: the silly games we invented as children or the wonderful holiday foods that Mom always prepared. Shared history, although not always pleasant, creates a special kind of intimacy. And as we grow older, we come to appreciate more and more what it means to have people in our lives who know us so completely.

The ties among family members are often so strong that we can't escape them, even if we want to. The familiar saying "Blood is thicker than water" refers to the incredible strength of familial relationships. You may not get along perfectly with one of your siblings—perhaps you were competitive as children, or perhaps you felt as though your parents always spoiled your younger brother without taking your feelings into account—but chances are, he or she is going to be a part of your life for the long haul. And for that reason, we need to learn to view all of our family ties as budding opportunities that, with care and attention, can flower into wonderful, mutually satisfying relationships. You may think that you have nothing in common with your siblings, or be critical of the choices they have made, but you will be surprised by the good feeling that comes from extending yourself to them and rekindling the connection among you. In the end, families not only offer us memories and a warm bed to sleep in when we pass through town—they provide us with a chance to learn to love others unconditionally, and to discover more about who we are.

Let Your Family Be Your Best Support System

I firmly believe that everything I've achieved in my life thus far is due, in no small part, to the fact that I was born into a strong, stable family. Over the years, whether I was competing in the Olympics or working to build my career as a motivational speaker, my father, mother, brothers, and sister have been an incredible support system for me. They have been there, offering love and encouragement, in my darkest hours and my brightest. And although all of our lives have changed significantly since the days when we sat together regularly at our dinner table in Fairmont, West Virginia, almost twenty years ago, the members of my family have been a constant source of strength that I rely on time and time again.

I know why families were created, with all their imperfections. They humanize you. They are made to make you forget yourself occasionally, so that the beautiful balance of life is not destroyed.

ANAÏS NIN

I'm the youngest of five children, and the baby of the family. I have three brothers, Ronnie, Donnie, and Jerry, and a sister, Shari. There's a seven-year difference between me and Ronnie, who's the oldest, but the five of us had a terrific time together growing up. Oh sure, we squabbled over things just like any other siblings—we fought over the favorite toys and over who got the last piece of Mom's chocolate cake. And of course, being the kid sister, I always wanted to tag along with the older kids. I was a real tomboy back then, and I was constantly trying to get my brothers to include me in their games and adventures.

Around the time I turned seven years old, my parents began exposing me to a wide range of activities, just as they'd done with my brothers and my sister before me. Having grown up running around the West

Virginia outdoors, we were an athletic bunch. In addition to taking gymnastics classes, I ran track, swam on the swim team, and was even a cheerleader. It seemed as if all of us were constantly being shuttled back and forth from one practice to another, but my parents never complained. They were just pleased that we were all so active, participating in healthy activities and developing real confidence in ourselves and in our abilities. But when I was twelve, I went to my mother and said, "I want to stop everything else and concentrate only on gymnastics." By that time, I knew two things: Gymnastics was what I loved the most and, clearly, it was what I did best. I had begun competing in competitions and I loved the rush of energy I got after putting on a great performance. My parents agreed that it was a good idea, and my mother was thrilled—from that point on, she only had to take me to *one* place after school!

As many opportunities as my parents gave us, they never pushed us into anything, and they never tried to live their lives through us. They let me discover my passion for gymnastics and then let me follow it as far as it would take me. Because of their generosity and unselfish love, I had the extraordinary experience of not only participating in the 1984 Summer Olympic Games in Los Angeles but of ultimately going all the way to win the gold medal in gymnastics as well. Only now, looking back, do I fully realize what an incredible gift my parents gave me when they allowed me to leave home, at the age of fourteen, and move to Houston to train with Bela Karolyi, the greatest women's gymnastics coach in the world—the man who'd trained my athletic role model, Nadia Comaneci.

I had patterned my athletic training after Nadia's ever since, as an eight-year-old stretched out in front of the television, I was mesmerized by a young Romanian girl and her gold medal performance in gymnastics at the 1976 Olympics in Montreal. Even now, I can still hear the words in my head as if I'd spoken them aloud: "I want to be like Nadia." And from that moment on, I absolutely believed that I would do it—that I would make it to the Olympics "like Nadia." But never, not even in the wildest moments of my admittedly vivid imagination, did I expect to have a chance to be trained by the man who had been Nadia's coach, the "mad Transylvanian," Bela Karolyi.

Bela first approached me after he saw me perform at a competition in Reno, Nevada. He walked right up to me, looked me in the eye, and said, "I'll make you into a champion." I was stunned. Did he mean *me?* And then he sat down with my parents and told them, "I think your daughter's got real potential." If it had been any other coach in the world, I think my parents would have been very resistant to the idea of my leaving home to train. I was their baby, after all, and I was still very young. But because it was *Bela,* because of his record and reputation, they took his offer seriously.

Back at home in West Virginia after the competition, I took some time off from the gym to think things over. Bela's offer meant the world to me—it meant that I actually might be able to go on to achieve my dream of competing at the Olympics—but I couldn't imagine moving to another city, or being away from my family and friends. The idea was exhilarating and terrifying at the same time. Nevertheless, I knew that I was standing on the cusp of a huge opportunity, and my parents knew it too. So it was during that time, the Christmas break of 1982, less than two years before the Olympic Games would open in Los Angeles, that we really discussed Bela's offer as a family.

I remember sitting together in our living room while the December snow fell softly and silently outside. I also remember that the television was off. That was a *big* deal. The television was always on in our house, but that day it stayed off because this was such an important decision. My mom and dad, being normal parents, were full of questions and concerns. But at the same time, they understood that this was my dream and my life. And so before they shared their own opinions, they asked me what *I* wanted to do. We all knew that I was at a crossroads in West Virginia. The coach I had was fantastic, but he'd taken me as far as he could, to a level where I just wasn't improving anymore. I'd made the Junior National Team and the coaches on the National Team had started talking about me: "That Retton kid might have what it takes." At that point, I usually finished fifth or sixth in the competitions; I was good, but very inconsistent. I'd score a 9.9 on vault and a 9.8 on the floor but then I'd fall three times off the beam. Even before Bela recruited me at the competition in Reno, I realized that if I wanted to reach that next level, I'd definitely have to make a change. I knew my raw talent was there, but I needed the focus and discipline of training that only someone like Bela could provide.

Back then, I didn't appreciate the extent of the sacrifice they would be making if they agreed to let me go by myself. As a parent, one of your greatest joys is watching your children grow and learn, sharing in not only their first steps but in other important milestones such as their first A on a math test, their first run scored in Little League baseball, or their first date. My parents would be missing out on some of that joy. They would also be, in a sense, turning me over to somebody else to raise. Mom and Dad had such particular ideas about child-rearing, and they were determined that I grow up with the same strong set of values that my other siblings had been raised with. I can only imagine how hard it must have been for them to even think about entrusting me to someone else's care at such a pivotol point in my life. Of course they could have just said no and that would have been the end of it. But once they heard me voice my hopes, they recognized that, by saying no, they might very well be standing in the way of what could turn out to be the greatest opportunity of my life. I remember my mom saying that if I wanted her to, she would even move to Houston with me. It was an extraordinary offer. But I said, "No, Mom, I can do this on my own. You've got four other kids at home who need you." I really believed I could do it myself, but I had no clue just how difficult it would be. I was very scared, yet at the same time, I was more excited than I had ever been before in my entire life.

Finally, after several hours of discussion, I took a deep breath and told them definitively that I wanted to give it a try. I was certain of this much: I didn't want to spend the rest of my life wondering "What if?" What if I never made it to the Olympics simply because I hadn't made the brave choice to train with Bela?

And my parents agreed.

Now, I have to be honest. I'm not sure that if either of my daughters come to me at the age of fourteen with a similar request, I'll be unselfish enough to do what my folks did for me. I'd certainly like to think so, but you never know. Either way, my own parents have provided an amazing model of what a family can be for all of us if we let it—an unwavering source of unconditional support and love that gives its members a firm foundation from which to pursue their own dreams and goals.

My parents' love for me was the reason I made it to the Olympics, pure and simple. And throughout my life, I have continued to turn to my family for encouragement and understanding as I face new opportunities and challenges—whether they be in my career or in raising my two daughters. The first step in cultivating truly rewarding family relationships is to recognize the potential love and support our family members have to offer, and make a commitment to reach out to them with open hearts and open minds. In doing so, we open the door to happiness, and the security and contentment that come with knowing that someone loves us for who we really are.

What You Make of Your Family Is Up to You

Now that I have my own family to look after and my own children to bring up, I'm making a real effort to provide the same kind of nurturing and supportive family unit for my husband and children that I had growing up. Outside of my relationship with God, the most important thing in the world to me is that my children and husband know that I love them with all my heart and that they can rely on me, whatever situations may arise. I always make time for fun activities with my girls despite my busy schedule, and every day I try to be sure that I hear the details of their days at school, or say their prayers with them at night. I do all this because the truth is that an ideal family is not something that we are simply born into—it's something that every single family member has to work at every day to create.

Even families with very similar circumstances to ours can suffer tremendous strife and unhappiness if family members refuse to treat each other with respect and choose to act selfishly instead of generously. My parents never tried to control me in the way that so many mothers and fathers of young athletes do. They weren't trying to build names for themselves or get their pictures in major magazines through me. They understood that my success was simply that: *my* success. And they never viewed my success as a key to their own happiness. At seventeen, I petitioned the court to become an adult so that I could assume control over my finances and put more money into a retirement plan. Again, unlike the parents of many young athletes, my parents didn't oppose it for a second because they believed that everything I'd earned was mine. Of course, that always made me *want* to do nice things for them, precisely because they never acted as if it was my obligation to do so.

The lesson here is clear: We all have a choice in how we treat those who are close to us. Making the right or wrong decisions about how to behave can either draw your family closer together, or drive a wedge between you that may be permanent. In Luke 6:31, Jesus urged his disciples to follow a general rule of thumb, which applies to all of our relationships and not just to those we share with family: "Do to others as you would have them do to you." This means giving the members of your family the same unconditional love and generosity that you seek from them. Think hard about your actions before you take them and look ahead to the long-term results: Will your behavior damage the trust that exists between you or prevent such a bond from existing in the future? No matter the situation, good intentions and kind behavior will go a long way toward fostering the type of fulfilling family relationship that will take you through the gateway to happiness.

Family relationships come in all shapes and sizes, and it's important to remember that, like all of our relationships, they will grow and change over the years. Hopefully, they change for the better. But you may find that you encounter some rough patches with a sibling or relative from time to time when one of you goes through a difficult period, or when distance and hectic schedules prevent you from keeping in touch as well as you might. Or perhaps an argument evolves into a deep-seated grudge that slowly pushes you farther apart and you feel as if you'll never see eye-to-eye again. When this happens, it is important that you continue to nurture the relationship with kindness and love. Even if the gesture isn't immediately returned, chances are that your differences will diminish over time and eventually the relationship will be repaired.

Although my sister Shari and I have always gotten along well, we were definitely not as close when we were growing up as we are today. I credit the strength of our current relationship with the consistent effort that we have both made, even when we were hundreds of miles apart, to talk regularly and share our experiences, goals, hopes, and fears. It took us a while to get to this point. Shari is five years older than I am, and growing up we didn't have much to talk about, other than our everyday childhood games, which she grew out of before I did. As I got older, I focused more and more on gymnastics and then left for Houston before I could begin to confide in her about normal teenage girl issues such as high school activities and boys. As sisters who saw each other regularly at family gatherings and of course shared much of the same history, we maintained an illusion of closeness. But in reality we knew very little about each other's lives, and I was much more likely to turn to my friends, or to Shannon, if I had a problem than to Shari.

But as we grew older, I began to realize what a wonderful, supportive resource I actually had in Shari. Here was somebody who knew all my quirks and pet peeves, and who intuitively understood my frame of reference for viewing the world because much of it overlapped with *her* frame of reference. We started chatting more frequently over the phone, and in the years since then she has become much more to me than a sister—she is one of my most treasured, dearest friends. We've coached each other through our pregnancies, through difficult job transitions and work-related crises, through health challenges and emotional bumps with other family members. I know that I can say anything to her, and I value our friendship—our *sisterhood*—tremendously.

It's amazing how family relationships can grow and thrive with a little nurturing. It would have been easy for me and Shari to continue on as blood relatives and little more; it's not as if there was ever any bad feeling between us and we'd always had a solidarity that came from being the two girls in a house full of boys. But what we have developed, with patience and time and effort, is worth so much more.

Our road was fairly easy, but even if you have a long-standing conflict with a parent or sibling—you don't approve of their spouse, they borrow money from you and never pay it back, you don't feel that they have supported your goals and ambitions in the past—you can work through it and build a stronger relationship if you just give it a shot. Talk to them with an open heart and listen with an open mind. Try to find common ground and see them for who they are—another human being, fallible, just like you. Forgive past mistakes and look to the future. It may take a long time, and you may never consider them your best friend, but easing the negative tensions between you will bring new sparkle to your life, and to theirs. Your other family members will thank you for it as well.

Sadly, these days with so many families spread out around the country, it's not always possible to have the safe, idealistic nuclear family that we all crave. Many people feel irreconcilably estranged from their parents and relatives, and don't feel that they have a reliable home base to fall back on in times of need. If this is the case with you, you may have to start from scratch with your spouse and build your own family. Or, you may find that there are other people whom you trust and with whom you feel you can share the same kind of unconditional love and acceptance. It's also important to realize that families aren't necessarily limited to just parents, children, and other immediate relatives. While there's no substitute for real blood lines, if you make the effort, you can find family everywhere you go.

During the two years I was in Houston training with Bela for the Olympics, I lived with a family named Spiller. One of their daughters, Paige, was also in Bela's group of elite gymnasts. They'd housed other young gymnasts before and so were very knowledgeable about the rigors of the training regimen I'd be going through. Bela's training was much harder than anything I'd ever done back in West Virginia and, especially during those first few months away from home, the Spillers provided an incredible support system for me. Even though my mother wrote me literally every day, I was still very homesick, crying and wanting to go home. And the Spillers were just wonderful, so loving and understanding about what I was going through. They treated me just like their other children and, for those two years that I was away, they became my surrogate family.

In fact, shortly after I arrived in Houston, Mrs. Spiller took Paige and me to get our ears pierced. All you female readers out there understand the significance of ear piercing—it's practically a rite of passage for young girls! So Paige and I were simply beside ourselves with anticipation, imagining all the pretty earrings we would buy. But as it happened, I neglected to tell Mrs. Spiller one small detail: My parents had forbidden me to get my ears pierced until I was eighteen. I suppose it was a little bit of rebelliousness on my part. But what I remember most clearly about the entire venture was the feeling it gave me of really *belonging* to the Spiller family. I had become their fifth child, and that sense of love and protection sustained me along the long, exhausting, and often trying road to the Olympics.

Even now, years later, when I manage to see my real family quite often and of course have Shannon and the girls, I am still in close contact with the Spillers. They remain some of my most cherished friends, and I continue to consider them a part of my extended family. In 1990, when Shannon and I were married, the Spiller family sent me this poem as a wedding gift:

A *little girl came to our house one day*
To find a place to stay
So that she could fulfill her dreams.
She was frightened but being the brave soul she is

She never let it be known.
She became a member of our family
She could gnaw a chicken leg to the bone
And handle a house full of rowdy boys.
This young girl brought with her
A heart full of love
And we had the love to return.
She left us one day
When her dream came true
We missed her more than she realized.
Now she is grown and soon to be married;
We were truly blessed to have had Mary Lou in our lives.

Reading this poem brought tears to my eyes. It all came rushing back to me—how the dear Spillers had welcomed me into their home and given me the strength and love I needed to achieve my dream. It just goes to show that family can be found in unexpected places and unexpected people—I mean, who ever imagined that I would travel halfway across the country and find a second family in Houston, Texas? Even if you feel that you are alone in the world, as all of us inevitably do at one point, if you open your heart to the people around you, you may find that family comes to you.

Balancing Your Family with Your Career

It's been sixteen years since the American flag was raised above our heads—mine and my teammates—at Pauley Pavilion in Los Angeles, signifying our gold medal triumph. Since then, I've married a wonderful man, Shannon Kelley, who is a successful investment broker. And I've become the mother of two daughters—Shayla, who's four, and

McKenna, who's two. When Shayla was born, I didn't think I could love anyone or anything as much as I loved her. But then, the same was true with McKenna when she was born two years later. I love my husband more than life itself, but I feel a different bond with my children. After Shayla was born, I found myself waking up in the middle of the night and tiptoeing my way down the darkened hall to the crib to watch her sleep. Children are a fundamental part of any family. They bring lightheartedness to those around them and communicate, even as newborns, an incredible enthusiasm for life. You may step on a toy at two in the morning when you're going to the bathroom, but if you're a parent, you don't care. That's what makes a house a home.

Now it's certainly no secret that I've worked hard my entire life to achieve success, and there's no doubt that success is rewarding. But success alone will not bring you happiness. To be truly happy we also need the time to enjoy—and be enjoyed by—the special people in our life. Few things are more fulfilling than the hours we spend talking, laughing, and sharing experiences with our family and friends. These are the moments that we remember most vividly and keep close to us throughout the years: The snowball fight that erupted in the backyard as the kids were helping you shovel the first snow; teaching your daughter to play the piano and watching those tiny hands struggle to reach from middle C all the way up to high C; or tossing the football with the boys in the backyard. If we're not careful we can easily lose sight of how precious the times with our family really are.

In addition to serving God faithfully, my top two priorities right

I looked on child rearing not only as a work of love and duty but as a profession that was fully interesting and challenging as any honorable profession in the world and one that demanded the best that I could bring to it.

ROSE KENNEDY

now are being a good mother and a good wife. Anything else, no matter how exciting and challenging it may be, can only make it as high as third place on my list of life's priorities. Many women today put off having children so they can invest their energy in getting their careers going. But the career may never be going well enough, and there may never be a time that seems exactly right. When Shannon and I got married, I decided that I didn't want my career to dictate when we had children. I wanted to have children when we *wanted* children—and so we did. I feel that my work schedule needs to revolve around *them*, as it will continue to do when—the Lord willing—we have more!

Being a mother is an incredibly rewarding experience because it teaches you to think of someone else first, rather than of yourself. During my athletic career, life was all about "me, me, me" and everything I did was geared toward achieving my goals and dreams. But when you're a mother, you quickly discover that your children's needs can't take second place to yours. You can't say to your six-month-old, "Don't worry, sweetie. Mommy will feed you tonight when she gets home from gymnastics practice." That's the kind of sacrifice you have to make as a parent, but in the end, the joy that you derive from the smile on your baby's face makes it well worth it.

My mother is a very strong Christian woman and she raised all of her kids that way. We were brought up with solid morals and wonderful values, and overall, she and my father did a terrific job. But their parental roles were pretty sharply divided. Dad was the provider in our family. He didn't work in the coal mines, but his work was coal mine–related: he fixed the transportation cables on the cars that took the workers down into the mines. Some of my earliest memories are of him coming home from work completely dirty and grimy from the coal soot. He would shower, eat the dinner my mother had prepared, and then lie on the couch for the rest of the evening watching television. He helped with absolutely nothing around the house and I remember my mom saying that he didn't change one diaper on five kids. But my mom was very old-fashioned. She felt that changing diapers was her job because she didn't work at a nine to five job like Dad did. It wasn't his responsibility to help with the children and housework.

Growing up, I heard a lot from my mom about a wife's duty to cook and clean and, truth be told, I enjoy doing those things. I take pride in the way our home looks, and I love cooking up a big dinner with a special dessert for Shannon and the kids. But my mom still believes that's the wife's only job, and I think a little differently. Like most women today, I'm also a career woman. The balance between my family, who always come first, and my career—a career that is, among other things, very important to the financial security of that family—is something I work hard to maintain. There've been some tough questions I've had to deal with along the way. How do I balance a demanding job and a family and keep it all together? How do I make sure that my children know they come first in my life? How do I live with the guilt of saying good-bye each morning to those sweet little faces when they don't understand where you go or why? All they want is for Mom to stay home and play. My husband doesn't experience the same kind of guilt. I don't think men instinctively feel the tug on the heartstrings the same way that mothers do when their children are confused or unhappy. It's not that I wish feelings of guilt on my husband—I certainly don't. I just have to remind myself that the kids do adjust to my being away part of the day and my work is important. Not only for the things it allows us to have as a family but for what it does for me, personally, to make me a more complete and fulfilled human being. A happier human being. And it goes without saying that the more confident I feel about my choices and my life, the more I'll be able to provide my daughters with the confidence *they* need to grow into proud, strong, intelligent young women.

I certainly don't mean to suggest that having a career is essential to someone's happiness. It's not. The woman (and even some men) that I know who have elected to be stay-at-home parents are extremely happy. But if you do continue to work after you and your spouse have children, it will take some serious effort on your part to ensure that your family unit stays close and connected and that your children continue to get the love and attention they require. And it's not easy to juggle everything—believe me, I know. But in the end, if you choose to have both a career and a family, it's a balance you have to strike.

One of the ways I maintain the balance between my family and my career is to give 110 percent of myself in everything I do. That's how I was raised by my parents, and it's how I was trained by my Bela. As an adult, I've been able to discipline myself to keep up this philosophy, and it's the way I'm raising my own children. By "giving 110 percent" I don't mean working yourself to the bone until you collapse from exhaustion—I simply mean being fully present and involved with whatever you are doing, when you are doing it. When I'm in another city giving a speech to a corporation, I give it my all. I focus completely on the job at hand: what I'm going to say, how I'm going to say it, and the issues and questions that are of importance to the group I'm addressing. When I'm there, I'm really there—I'm not on the cell phone to the kids or planning next week's meals in the back of my mind. But the second I'm through speaking, or shooting a commercial, or whatever it is that my work involves that day, all I think about is getting home to my family. I call Shannon and the girls from the car on my way to the airport. From that point on, I'm "Mom" again, listening to what Shayla did in preschool or how McKenna dressed up her Barbie that day. There's no jotting down a memo to my manager while absentmindedly listening to Shayla talk about her upcoming school play. I am completely focused on the members of my family, giving them all the love and attention they need.

Shayla has recently become more vocal with regard to her feelings about my leaving for work every day, and particularly concerning my more extended trips. If you're a parent you've heard something similar. "Why are you leaving?" "Do you have to go?" "Wouldn't you rather stay home and play with me?" Of course, when she says these things, she might as well take my heart right out of my chest and squeeze! Like any working parent, I feel terribly guilty each time I have to put my foot down and explain, that no, Mommy has to go. And children learn very quickly exactly which buttons to push.

When my kids are unhappy about my leaving, I try to turn their feelings completely around. Instead of responding to their pleas with apologies, I try to make my work sound intriguing and exciting. I let them know that Mommy is having fun doing something wonderful that they aren't allowed to do—yet. As my children grow older, I feel it's extremely important to make them understand just how much Mommy loves her work. I want them to realize that through hard work and a good education they, too, can become anything they choose. Recently Shayla informed me she's going to be a "fire girl" and McKenna intends to become a "police girl." How great is that! Gone are the days of stereotypes and limitations for girls and women in their career choices. I want my daughters to grow up respecting their working mom, to be proud of me and view me as their role model. But that won't happen if they feel in any way that my career detracted from my role as their mother and their biggest source of support and understanding—and that's exactly why balancing your job and your family is so incredibly important.

Spending quality time with our children on their level is one of the most important things Shannon and I can do as parents to ensure that they're getting the attention they need and that we continue to build strong parent-child relationships. By getting down to their level,

I mean literally getting down on the floor (which for me at four foot nine is not too hard) and playing with them. Just playing whatever they want to play.

My oldest daughter, Shayla, is a very bright, high-energy little girl. She was two when her baby sister, McKenna, was born, and from the outset, she was extremely jealous. So I made an extra effort to spend quality time with her alone. No one else, just Mommy and Shayla. We had this special time when McKenna went down for her afternoon nap. I would ask, "Okay, Shayla, what would you like to do during our special time?" Her reply was always the same: "Mommy, I want to play with your fer-fume!" And even though I'd be thinking, "No, please, not the perfume again," I'd say, "Okay, sweetheart, let's go!"

So there I'd be, every day, down on the floor in my bathroom, playing with my daughter and my silver tray of perfume bottles. Shayla liked to pretend that the pretty colored bottles were babies. We'd wrap the bottles up with blankets (tissues) and, if they happened to have a "boo-boo," we'd put small pieces of torn masking tape on them as bandages. Then we'd feed the "babies" their bottles (which were actually my lipsticks) or change their diapers (I always bought extra toilet paper for our diapering service). We played for hours until the real baby woke up.

I also used our special time alone to try to introduce the Lord to Shayla in very small ways. I told her that God loved her and that He gave her such a beautiful baby sister because she is so special in His eyes. This was a particularly important idea for me to communicate because Shayla was so jealous of her new sister. At that point, she was refusing to participate with the baby in any way. When I finished nursing, I tried to get her to help me feed the baby a bottle, a job that many little girls love. Nope, she didn't want any part of that. I asked her to go and retrieve diapers for me as "Mommy's helper." "You do it,

Mommy." Did she want to hold the baby? Not a chance. I was feeling so afraid and confused because I wanted her to love and adore her baby sister and clearly she didn't. However, seeing her on my bathroom floor with my perfume bottles, singing to them, feeding them, changing and loving them, rocking them to sleep, I realized what a beautiful heart she had. All the things she saw me doing for her and her new baby sister, she was acting out on my perfume bottles.

A few months later, while sitting on my bathroom floor once again playing "fer-fume," Shayla was rocking one of her "babies" to sleep. I asked, " Oh, your baby is so cute, what's her name?" Her answer took me so totally by surprise that I started to cry. "McKenna," she said. "God gave her to me because I'm so special." She'd heard me! I hadn't been wasting my breath all this time! It was a moment I'll always treasure. I knew then how priceless those hours on the bathroom floor had been. By spending that quality time with Shayla, I was able to help her work through her jealousy and strengthen the bond between us to the point where she no longer felt threatened. It wasn't long before she started to direct those kind and loving feelings toward McKenna, and now they're as close as can be.

One thing that has helped me and Shannon tremendously in maintaining the delicate balance between career and family is to map out our priorities and figure out exactly when is work time and when is family time. Not long ago I made a major change in my professional life that resulted in my taking on more responsibility for the day-to-day management of my own career. It was an important decision that also required me to make some pretty significant lifestyle changes, so after it happened, Shannon and I sat down and discussed how to best incorporate my new role into our family life. We came up with a pretty effective plan. Naturally, it won't work for everybody, as each family is as unique as the people in it, but it works for us:

- Our children attend preschool three days a week for a few hours in the morning, which is when I get the majority of my office work done. But the minute I'm back in the carpool lane waiting to pick them up from preschool, I'm back to being Mom.

- After 4 P.M., I don't answer the telephone. From that hour until 7:30 P.M. is the most hectic time in our home. I cook dinner and we eat; then Shannon does the dishes. Then there's bathtime, reading to the girls (two books each), prayers, and bedtime. It's a daily ritual we all cherish. I figure nothing is so important that it can't wait till morning. And if a work-related emergency does arise during their time, they're allowed into the office with me, but they know they need to remain quiet. I give them paper and markers and they do their "work" just as Mommy does. Sometimes I'll have them help me fax a document or put the stamp on a letter. The basic idea is that I always try to involve them in what I'm doing, so it doesn't detract from our time together.

- My rule on travel: I'm only gone one night and then it's back home for me. I always try to be home before 7:30 P.M. so I can read to the girls, say their prayers with them, and tuck them into bed. And yes, exceptions do occur. If I have to be somewhere longer than a day—say a week for a commercial shoot on location somewhere—I take them with me.

If you are a parent, I encourage you to work with your children and spouse to design a schedule that works for you and helps you hit that necessary balance. But even if you don't have children, it's helpful to have a clear idea of the time you want to devote to family members. All too often our busy days run away with us and we find that yet another week has passed without having lunch with our sister, as we'd intended. Or that we've barely crossed paths or really talked with our spouse, save for falling asleep together exhausted and burnt out at night. Paying close attention to our daily routine helps us to make sure that by the week's end, we've made ample time for the people who are really important. Remember, no one on their deathbed ever says, "I wish I'd spent more time at the office."

One of my very favorite passages from the Bible is Proverbs 31: 10–31, entitled "The Wife of Noble Character."

THE WIFE OF NOBLE CHARACTER

A wife of noble character who can find? She is worth far more than rubies.

Her husband has full confidence in her and lacks nothing of value.

She brings him good, not harm, in all the days of her life.

She selects the wool and flax and works with eager hands.

She is like the merchant ships, bringing her food from afar.

She gets up while it is still dark: she provides food for her family and portions for her servant girls.

She considers a field and buys it: out of her earnings she plants a vineyard.

She sets about her work vigorously: her arms are strong for her tasks.

She sees that her trading is profitable, and her lamp does not go out at night.

In her hand she holds the distaff and grasps the spindle with her fingers.

She opens her arms to the poor and extends a hand to the needy.

When it snows, she has no fear for her household: for all of them are clothed in scarlet.

She makes coverings for her bed: she is clothed in fine linen and purple.

Her husband is respected at the city gate, where he takes his seat among elders of the land.

She makes linen garments and sells them, and supplies the merchants with sashes.

She is clothed with strength and dignity: she can laugh at the days to come.

She speaks with wisdom, and faithful instruction is on her tongue.

She watches over the affairs of her household and does not eat the bread of idleness.

Her children arise and call her blessed: Her husband also, and he praises her: Many women do noble things, but you surpass them all . . .

Give her the reward she has earned, and let her works bring her praise at the city gate.

This woman, the wife of noble character, is whom I strive to be every single day of my life: a hard worker who loves what she does, is respected in her community and gives something back to it, and, at the same time, is a loving homemaker who enjoys providing the day-to-day necessities for her family. Most important, she is a mother and a role model who keeps the family tightly knit, and whose children love and respect her. Nothing, not even a gold medal, has ever made me any happier.

Keeping Your Family Strong

As I mentioned earlier, keeping your family ties strong and satisfying requires consistent, well-intentioned effort on your part. You can't create a familial bond overnight, but you'll find that if you put in the energy, you'll be able to build some of the most uniquely fulfilling relationships you've ever had. Here are some good rules to keep in mind:

- *Be vocal about your affection*—Not everyone is accustomed to sharing their feelings and emotions out loud with others, but telling your loved ones how much you care for them is one simple way to enhance your family relationships. Because we are often in such close proximity with our families, we tend to overlook the need to verbalize our affection—but this easy gesture can lift another person's spirits or bridge a gap between family members who are estranged. Don't underestimate the power of words.

  Once, in the fourth or fifth grade, my homework assignment was to tell the members of my family that I loved them. I can still remember the day. My mom was in the kitchen and I was sitting on top of our breakfast table, which was a long wooden picnic table with benches. I was so nervous just having to say it. I knew I was loved—I knew that. But we just didn't verbalize it in my family. That day, I remember saying, "Mom, I love you," and then jumping off the table and running out of the room. It was a sort of drive-by loving. She called after me and said, "I love you too," also very fast. And that was it. There was no discussion about it, why I said it or anything else. We didn't even pause in our daily lives to enjoy the expression of the emotion or the good feeling that comes from saying those words.

  I learned an important lesson from that experience. I knew right then that I didn't want to raise my own children like that. From that moment on, I vowed to myself that I'd tell my kids "I love you" all the time. It's tremendously important to me that my kids know that they couldn't be loved any more than they are. My husband and I are almost corny on that point. We say "I love you" as easily as we say "hello" and the kids pick up on that. If you call our house and get our answering machine, Shayla says, "Hi, this is the Kelley house, we're not home so leave a message. I love you." And then McKenna chimes in with her own "I love you, bye-bye." Those words were their own idea, they just said them without any prompting from Shannon or me. I'm so proud of the fact that they can express their emotions openly.

- *Don't get caught up in petty disagreements* — Sadly, silly disagreements that aren't even worth the energy needed to have them are at the root of many family conflicts. We are conditioned to feel comfortable around family, but that can work to our disadvantage if we allow ourselves to lose our temper over minimal issues, or get pulled into futile arguments that we would never participate in with friends or coworkers. We can slip back into patterns with siblings that are left over from our childhood days, rather than behaving like mature adults. Family members know just how to push our buttons, it's true — but don't let petty scrapes undermine worthwhile relationships.

My parents still live in West Virginia, but Shannon and I are raising our family in Houston. The truth is that if I didn't call my parents periodically, I'd never hear from them. Although my three brothers all still live in West Virginia, and my sister lives relatively close by, in Pittsburgh, they, too, rarely speak with our folks on the telephone. My father simply doesn't like the phone, and doesn't use it unless he absolutely has to. And my mother will talk on the phone if someone calls her, but it doesn't really occur to her to pick up the phone and call someone for a chat. It may sound strange in this day and age, but that's how they feel and, being older, they're set in their ways.

By now I've gotten to a place where I've accepted the fact that this is just the way my parents are. It's not that they don't love me, or that they don't want to talk to us. Phone calls are just something I have to initiate.

There was a time when this genuinely bothered me. It was a phone call, after all—the phone was right there in the house, and I just couldn't get my head around what the big deal was. But then it eventually dawned on me that for over twenty-five years, my mother's life revolved around raising her five kids. She gave up so much of her life for us. She was a completely devoted mother; she did her job and she did it well. But now that she's done, she's busy enjoying doing things for herself. For the first time, doing what she enjoys, such as going to aerobics class and doting on her grandkids, can actually be her priority. She loves her life now and I'm happy for her. And the fact that she doesn't pick up the phone and call me regularly doesn't mean she loves me any less—it just means that she's doing her own thing.

It's taken me a while, but I've finally realized that if I want to talk to my mother, I need to call her. And that's okay—in God's grand scheme, it's a very small thing. And I can certainly do that much for the woman who has given me so much strength and affection throughout my life. Keeping in regular contact with my parents makes me very happy. Once I realized this, it didn't matter who called whom. My relationship with my family is simply too important for me to allow silly little things, petty issues and misunderstandings, to get in the way of our closeness. It's really no more complicated than that.

There's a great prayer that I always keep in mind when dealing with situations like this. Appropriately, it's called the Serenity Prayer:

God, grant me the courage to change the things I
cannot accept,
the strength to accept the things I cannot change,
and the wisdom to know the difference between the two.

And you know what? Now when I call home, my mother ends every conversation with "I love you" and she gets the same response back from me. Some things do change!

- *Appreciate your loved ones while you can*—When we get wrapped up in achieving our goals, we sometimes forget to take the time to enjoy the people we love. Too often it takes a serious incident or loss to put our lives into perspective.

When I was eighteen, I lost my biggest fan: my Grandfather Retton. It was just a few years after the Olympics and he'd been sick for a long time. He'd had several heart attacks, and had suffered for years with severe Parkinson's disease. I was just so glad that he lived long enough to watch me at the Olympics—that was his dream. My grandfather was the first person I'd ever lost who was close to me and, when he died, it was also the first time I ever saw my dad cry. It was his father. As a kid, Grandpa is Grandpa, but you don't really see Grandpa as being someone's dad. That experience made me appreciate how God has blessed my parents, my siblings, my husband and my children, with good health. They are the keys to my happiness, now and always, and every day I try to remind myself of how blessed I have been to have them in my life, and to make the most of our time together. My friend Michael Jordan once offered me a poignant reminder that we never know when a loved one may be taken away and that we need to enjoy them every day of our lives.

Michael Jordan and I go way back. We first met at the 1984 Olympic Games in Los Angeles, where he was a hotshot college basketball player from North Carolina and I was a wide-eyed teenager from West Virginia. We both left Los Angeles with gold medals and he won another in 1992 with the original Dream Team.

Michael once told me something very important about the necessity of appreciating your loved ones while you can. In 1996 I was writing my column for *USA Today* at the Summer Games in Atlanta. Michael had recently lost his father in a horrible way—two young men shot him in cold blood so they could steal his car. I asked Michael how he could even begin to deal with the pain and the loss, and I'll never forget what he told me. He said, "From the death of my father, I took a positive. Hey, I had him for thirty-one years. Some people never had their father for two or three years. He was able to mold me into a mature young man who could make decisions for myself."

Michael's strength during a terribly difficult time stemmed from the fact that he knew he and his father had had a full life together. He felt positive about their relationship, and his memories and the lessons that his father had taught him stayed with him and pulled him through. We always want more time with our loved ones than God gives us, but knowing that we made our very best efforts to be actively involved in their lives will give us comfort should we lose them before their time. I so admire Michael for his dignity and for his faith. And he's so right. The happiness we take from our family members doesn't end when they leave us. Especially if we've told them how much we loved them while they were here.

So reach out to a loved one today. Make plans with your

family. If they live far away, call them at least once a week. E-mail is a quick and easy way to stay in close contact, and the Internet provides a perfect medium to share family photographs or your child's first artistic masterpieces with relatives who live far away. Remember birthdays and anniversaries; mark them on your calendar and follow through with a card or note. Send cookies to your children who are away at school or fresh flowers to your grandmother with the green thumb. And pray for your family on a regular basis.

These seem like such simple gestures and they are. But that's also why they're so easy to overlook. So resolve not to let that happen! You'll be amazed at the good things that come to you and your family members as you open yourselves up, start sharing, and nurture the inimitable bonds between you. What awaits you is not only a new kind of happiness, but a never-ending wellspring of love, support, trust, and companionship.

THE SECOND GATEWAY

Faith

The care of God for us is a great thing,
if a man believe it at heart, it plucks
the burden of sorrow from him.

EURIPIDES

Since the world began, man has endeavored to solve the mystery of his own existence. We look up into the bright blue expanse of sky that hangs above our heads and wonder what secrets lie behind the stars, and how it happened that we are here on this earth, able to walk, talk, laugh, and breathe. We marvel at the miracle of life each time a baby is born, and give deep thanks for life's blessings and memories when a loved one passes away. Being human means being curious about the world around us. It is our very nature to passionately ask questions about the purpose of our lives, and ponder what unseen forces shape our experiences, the good and the bad. As we go about our daily routines, fulfilling our roles as spouses, coworkers, parents, and friends, we long to find a source of comfort and certainty in the vastness of the great, wide universe.

For many people, the answers to life's deepest questions can be found through spiritual faith. Faith is what renowned naturalist and writer Terry Tempest Williams describes as "a teacher in the absence of fact"—it fills in the gaps in our understanding and answers questions that science can't explain. Faith is the belief in an all-knowing God whose wisdom is superior to our own. And it conveys the experience of placing your trust in His divine wisdom and choosing to accept and embrace Him as a constant source of guidance and inspiration.

Faith is a gateway to happiness that remains permanently accessible to each of us, wherever we are, no matter our circumstances. Like the lighthouse perched on rocky cliffs that steers lonely ships safely back to shore, faith can guide us to make better choices, become better individuals, and find our way to true happiness. Faith allows us to have a deep, personal relationship with our Creator and to explore the intricacies of our own souls. It is an unending supply of joy and sustenance that can help us through our darkest moments and open the door to lasting peace and fulfillment.

I've been a "pleaser" my whole life. I've always been the "good girl," someone who avoids any kind of confrontation, anything that might spark controversy or ruffle people's feathers. I'm certainly no psychologist, but I'm sure this tendency to please everyone has something to do with the home environment into which I was born. When you're the youngest—and the smallest—you work harder to be noticed, ideally in a positive way. I always made an effort to be the "good" child, the one who stood out from the crowd because she did absolutely everything that was expected of her.

I think that much of my lifelong eagerness to please has to do with the fact that I entered the public arena at such a young age. As members of the Olympic team, my teammates and I faced tremendous pressure to give a stellar performance and bring home the gold medal. I always had older people—coaches, managers, agents, accountants, publicists—advising me about everything: where to go, what to say, and how and when to say it. I generally shied away from putting in my own two cents and I almost never argued with anyone or expressed my own opinion. The reason: I was terribly afraid of saying the wrong thing, or that people would be disappointed or stop liking me if I did.

Now don't get me wrong, most of the advice I received growing up was very good advice. My life and career have definitely benefited from all the loving guidance and support I've received from so many. But as an adult, I've come to recognize that because I never wanted to "rock the boat" most people assumed that I didn't have any strong opinions or beliefs of my own, which certainly has never been the case. (Just ask my husband!)

When I sat down to write this book, I realized that it wouldn't be possible for me to be completely honest about my life and my gateways to happiness without running the risk of not "pleasing" some people. For example, I immediately understood that by identifying "Faith" as one of my gateways I might upset—even anger—some people. Perhaps they'd think I was proselytizing on behalf of my own religious beliefs, preaching some kind of "Gospel According to Mary Lou." Who is *she* to tell me what to believe? Furthermore, faith is a very private matter, and some people might not be comfortable with my discussing their beliefs on the pages of this book. These questions worried me a lot. To tell you the truth, I prayed about them.

Sometimes our prayers are answered in totally unexpected ways. My response quite literally arrived in the mail. It came in the form of a letter asking me to participate—for the first time—in one of Dr. Billy Graham's Crusade for Christ events. Like the many other athletes and celebrities who had spoken at previous Crusades, I'd been invited to become a "witness" for Christ and to offer personal testimony about the role He plays in my life.

I was overwhelmed and honored by the invitation. I have always believed that Billy Graham is one of God's angels on this earth. He has personally ministered to every U.S. president since Harry Truman and through his Crusades (which are now held in football-size arenas, often over multiple nights), he has carried the Word of Christ to millions of people in every corner of the globe for more than fifty years. He is a compassionate, honest, inspiring man who has helped countless individuals find faith and improve their lives by turning to God.

But as thrilled as I was by the prospect of meeting and working with him firsthand, I hesitated. Over forty thousand people were expected to attend and the entire program would be taped for a later television broadcast. It would be a high-profile event with a lot of media in attendance. If I were to stand at that microphone as a witness for Christ, it would mean that I'd chosen to start down a road from which there would be no turning back.

It's not that I had any reluctance to talk about my faith. Just the opposite, in fact. My Christian faith is the cornerstone of everything in my life, and I'd always been willing to talk openly about it with anyone who asked. Prior to this, however, those conversations usually were in small groups or on a one-to-one basis with a friend. And although I had spoken before some Baptist gatherings in the past, this was by far the largest platform I'd ever been given from which to speak publicly about my relationship with Jesus Christ.

Shannon and I spent hours talking it over, weighing the pros and cons of accepting Dr. Graham's invitation. In my heart, there was no question that I wanted to do it. But in my mind all I heard were the words of Mary Lou the pleaser—and she wasn't pleased. "Are you crazy?" demanded the worried voice inside my head. "Don't you realize that the quickest way to make enemies is by taking a stand on politics or religion? That's not your job."

I wavered back and forth trying to make a decision. I really didn't know what to do. Then, out of nowhere, Shannon started to smile, as if he'd just remembered the right answer to a million-dollar question. Excitedly, he asked me, "Honey, where did you say this Crusade was going to be held?"

"St. Louis," I replied, wondering why this piece of information was suddenly so important.

His smile turned into a full-blown grin. He looked at me and said, "You know how some cities have nicknames, like New York is the Big Apple and Philadelphia is the City of Brotherly Love?"

"Sure . . ." I said, hesitantly. The puzzled look on my face made it obvious that I had no idea what he was talking about.

"Do you know what the nickname for St. Louis is?" he asked.

I didn't. I shook my head no.

"St. Louis is known as the Gateway City."

The Gateway City. I had prayed earnestly for guidance about what to do, and now that guidance was unfolding here before me. Talk about being given a sign! As soon as Shannon said the words "Gateway City," all my doubts were instantly resolved. I felt as if I'd been sent a giant neon arrow that was pointing directly toward St. Louis. And I knew in my heart that the questions of faith were inextricably linked to the message in this book.

Participating in Dr. Graham's Crusade turned out to be one of the most extraordinary experiences of my life. Although dozens of people ask for "just five minutes" of his time (and believe me, I know how quickly those can add up), Dr. Graham was gracious enough to invite Shannon and me to his dressing room for a brief visit before the event began. Earlier that day, I had made the decision that if the opportunity presented itself, I would summon up my courage and ask Billy Graham for some spiritual advice. After all, how often do you have the opportunity to tap the wisdom of one of the country's greatest spiritual leaders? Of course the question I most wanted to ask him was, "How can I talk honestly about my faith without seeming to be judgmental of those who don't share my belief?"

We arrived backstage and were ushered into Dr. Graham's dressing room. A moment later we were in the presence of the man whom President Bush once described as "one of God's true warriors." He greeted us warmly and then introduced us to his son, Franklin, who had just returned from ministering to victims of a terrible earthquake in Turkey. We talked about Franklin's work and then we spoke briefly about the evening's program.

At this point, I sensed that our visit was about over. He'd already given us more time than we expected. We started walking toward the door and I knew it was now or never, so I seized the moment.

"Excuse me, Dr. Graham," I said, hesitating. "But I was just wondering if . . . I have a question I wanted to ask you."

He stopped walking and looked directly at me, giving me his full attention. The kindness in his eyes made my nervousness disappear. "I'm writing a book about finding happiness," I told him. "And I have a chapter in it on faith. How do I get my message across to those who don't know Him?"

Dr. Graham's response was immediate. "You can't make people believe in God," he said. "You can only live your life as best you can and have it be an example for others. Hopefully, they will see the difference between how you live your life and how they live theirs. It's the Holy Spirit that changes people, not you. They first have to be willing to let Him into their hearts."

I thanked him profusely and once again we started moving toward the door. Just before saying good-bye, he added one final comment: "You know, I just got back from talking with some students at Harvard. And many of them had the same question you did. I told them what I just told you: Live by example."

So let me start off by being clear. Jesus Christ is my Lord and Savior. Every day, through knowing Him, I experience the deepest kind of happiness I've ever had. It's a happiness that requires only one thing from me: my total faith and belief in Him.

At the same time, I want to make it equally clear that I am not trying to force my personal beliefs on anyone. Even though I've found complete happiness through my faith in Christ, I'm certainly not suggesting that if you don't share my belief you can't be happy. My purpose here isn't to preach. All I hope is that by sharing the experience of my own faith and the happiness it provides me on a daily basis, I will inspire you to consider the idea of faith and the role it can play in bringing happiness and fulfillment to your life as well.

My one purpose in life is to help people find a personal relationship with God, which, I believe, comes through knowing Christ.

THE REVEREND
BILLY GRAHAM

Finding Your Faith

The issue of faith is a deeply personal one for most people, and each individual's conception of faith is completely unique to him or her. Although the Bible offers some basic guidelines, God works in different ways in the lives of His children. How you relate to God and find your faith will be different from everyone else's story, as is how you choose to practice it day to day. Finding our way to faith requires that we ask ourselves some difficult but vitally important questions about what we believe and how we want to express those beliefs. It requires a totally unique kind of trust and commitment that we seldom experience in our interpersonal relationships but that are vital to cultivating a fulfilling relationship with God. And because of the experiences of my own life, I think I've developed a much better understanding of how true that really is.

I was brought up in a very devout Catholic household. All five kids went to Catholic Sunday school and our entire family attended Mass together every week. When I was a child, I witnessed the depth of my mother's faith on a daily basis, along with the happiness it obviously brought to her life. Her heartfelt belief in the Church, its teachings and traditions, its rituals and its structure, also left a powerful impression on me. She was so determined to teach us the importance of practicing faith that every year during Lent she took my brothers, my sister, and me to Mass before school each day. When you consider that Lent lasts for forty days, you'll have an idea about the level of my mother's commitment to giving us a good Catholic upbringing!

I had always followed closely in my mother's religious footsteps. I invited Jesus into my heart at an early age, and when I moved to Houston to train for the Olympics, I continued my secondary education at Northland Christian School. From childhood on up through my becoming a young adult, and even as a bonafide grown-up, I always remained very content and comfortable in my Catholicism. It never even occurred to me that there might be any alternative way for me to worship. As far as I knew, Catholicism *was* synonymous with faith.

It was only when I began my relationship with the man who would later become my husband, Shannon Kelley, that I first had any reason to even think about or question my Catholicism. One of the principal reasons I fell in love with Shannon when we first met during our days at the University of Texas was that right from the beginning of our relationship, I clearly saw the important role that faith played in his life. Even with the intense pressure from his studies and his demanding position as starting quarterback for the University of Texas Longhorns, Shannon's faith was always his top priority. There was one major difference between us, however. Unlike me, the good Catholic girl from West Virginia, Shannon found his gateway through the doors of the Baptist Church.

Shannon was the first Baptist I ever really got to know on a deep level. And despite what some people may believe, I never for a moment felt that it was wrong for me, a Catholic, to be dating him, a Protestant. Over time, as we came to know each other better, we shared a lot about our respective beliefs—where they were the same, where they differed. I was consistently impressed by the thoughtfulness and maturity he brought to our discussions. We're not too far apart in age (he's only three years older than I am), but quite often during those late night talks about God and our perception of Him, I felt as though he'd already spent a lifetime thinking about some of these ideas.

It wasn't until we'd known each other for quite a while that Shannon seemed to feel comfortable in talking openly with me about the details of his religious background. It turned out that his family situation had been entirely different from mine in terms of how they practiced their faith. Although they were Christians, Shannon's family weren't regular churchgoers, nor did they place much emphasis on instilling religious values in their children. I was amazed to discover that Shannon was actually envious of me because I had been brought up in a strongly religious household, even though it was a Catholic one.

Eventually, Shannon shared with me the remarkable personal journey that he'd taken in order to arrive at his faith. When he was fourteen years old, he had attended a fellowship camp for Christian Youth where he spent the summer learning about the Word of Christ and what His teachings and love could offer him. Even though he was still very young, the experience opened him up on a spiritual level and prompted him to invite Jesus Christ into his life and heart. Shannon returned home from camp so committed to his newfound faith that he persuaded his mother to drive him all over town just so he could find the best church to join. After attending several different types of services at churches of different denominations, he ended up choosing the Baptist Church

Over the course of our courtship, it started to become clear to me that I might have some choice in the way that I related to God. I began to realize that my personal faith wasn't rooted in any one denomination. I would always be a Christian, I knew that. But would I remain a Catholic?

For a long time, the answer to that question would be "yes." In 1990, after five years of dating, Shannon and I were married in a Catholic ceremony. A few years before, my big sister, Shari, had been married in the Church and following the tradition was important to me. At that point in my life, regardless of any questions I may have had about my own Catholic faith, I still couldn't imagine getting married anywhere else. Catholicism was a part of my personal history, and the familiar rituals made the celebration of our marriage all that more meaningful. It was something I wanted and, of course, it was something that I knew would make my family very happy. Shannon was incredibly understanding. We never quarreled about it, not once.

But after we'd crossed the threshold into our new life together, we both knew that we'd only deferred making a decision about our respective faiths. The love we shared and the commitment we'd made to each other wouldn't allow Shannon and me to spend our lives worshiping in separate churches. What would we do?

Well, for the first few years, we compromised. One Sunday we attended a Catholic church, the next Sunday, a Baptist church. Back and forth. Forth and back. But we both understood that this was only a short-term solution to our fundamental problem.

The situation finally came to a head when, after several years of marriage and of flip-flopping churches, Shannon and I began to discuss starting our own family. Our biggest concern for our future children was how we could best provide them with the same serious Christian foundation that had been so important, so essential, in both of our lives. We both felt that switching church services from week to week would be much too confusing for a child. So, after many long hours of intense discussion, I finally decided to follow my husband, the leader of our family, on what was, for me, a new path to a familiar destination. I became a member of the Baptist Church.

Was I afraid? You bet I was. Even though I never doubted the decision once I'd made it, there were still times when I worried that other people would think badly of me for it; that I'd be seen as a turn-coat, a betrayer of my parents' faith. And, as Mary Lou the pleaser, I knew that more than anything, my decision would greatly *displease* my mother. Thankfully—although it certainly took some time—she eventually came to respect my choice. She finally understood that I'd chosen this path because I needed to secure happiness for my own family, for my husband and for the children we still intended to raise and love with total faith in the Lord—just as she'd raised me. She recognized that I was still devoted to my faith but was choosing to embrace it in a different way.

It was a huge change for me, a giant step. There were times when I wondered if my faith would be weakened without some of the rituals and traditions, such as confession, that had been a major part of my life since I was a child. It wasn't that I ever believed I'd be out of God's sight if I wasn't engaged in the organized sitting, standing, and kneeling that accompanies Sunday Mass, or that He would no longer acknowledge me if lighting candles and speaking a little Latin ceased to be part of my worship experience. I was just nervous about making such a permanent change in the way I practiced my faith. Baptist worship was so different. When I first started attending the Baptist church, it seemed as if all they did was *sing*. I was moving out of my comfort zone and it was frightening. But once again, I ultimately found myself happier as a result. As soon as I committed to the Baptist Church, as soon as I gave myself over fully to the experience, it wasn't long before I found myself very much at home in my new church, enjoying the singing with ever-increasing vigor and discovering many new wonders in the ways of Baptist worship.

Quite unexpectedly, something else resulted from my decision to join the Baptist Church. I found a new identity—or perhaps I should say I came into an expanded identity and a deepening of my faith. I'm not a Catholic anymore but, even though I'm very happy in my new church, I've chosen not to identify myself as a Baptist either. Now I simply think of myself as a *Christian*. Period. When I say that, I'm certainly not criticizing people who consider themselves to be part of a single denomination. I myself did that for years. I'm only saying that it's no longer an issue for me. In looking to God for guidance and searching my own soul, I have found a new way to think about myself and my faith, one that works with my own needs and the needs of my family.

Finding your faith, much like finding happiness, is an ongoing journey that can take years or even, for some, an entire lifetime. Your faith may evolve and change as you change. The important thing is to grab hold of it and never let go. If you don't consider yourself a spiritual person, or haven't been raised to believe in a certain faith, there are many paths that you can take to learn more about the difference God can make in your life. One very helpful way is to look to spiritual role models—a clergyman or simply a friend whose devotion to faith you admire—and discuss your thoughts and listen to their counsel and experience. Their stories and wisdom can inspire you and help you make sense of the questions you may have.

The most important step toward finding your faith is to passionately ask yourself those soul-searching questions we all have and to give serious consideration to your answers. What do *you* have faith in? Do you believe that what you know through your five senses is all there is? Does science really explain everything for you—from the origins of life to the intricacies of the human heart? Do you think that this earthly existence is all we'll ever know?

I urge you to look deep into your heart for the answers to these questions, and to be honest with yourself about what you find. I believe that you'll come to believe what I already know—that God's infinite knowledge and compassion shines through everything that is mysterious and wonderful about our lives. By welcoming Him into our hearts, we light the way to a life of happiness that comes from knowing that we are a part of something much greater than ourselves.

Faith Is Not the End, It's the Beginning

One of my favorite passages from the Bible is Proverbs 3:5–6: "Trust in the Lord with all your heart and lean not on your own understanding:

in all your ways acknowledge Him, and He will make your paths straight." This verse always reminds me of the tattered and torn piece of paper I have taped to my office desk. It reads:

Good morning! This is God. I will be
Handling all your problems today.
I will not need your help. So have
a nice day.

Remember that wonderful Bobby McFerrin song "Don't Worry, Be Happy" from a few years back? The title describes with perfect simplicity the exhilarating happiness which comes from giving all your problems, your struggles, your *worries,* over to God. But while I'm certain that God put each one of us on this earth for a purpose, I also believe that He gives us the free will to choose our own path. He puts us in situations, gives us certain talents, and then lets us make our own choices about what to do. Faith and our trust in God are never an excuse for abandoning personal responsibility—it's merely the jumping-off point from which we can begin to make decisions that will help us build lives that we love. Faith will eventually lead a person to happiness, but never without some effort on his or her part as well.

I don't think God made me go to Houston, which was probably the most important decision of my life. He gave me the opportunity, but ultimately it was my choice and my parents' choice whether or not I would accept Bela's offer. I'm convinced that there was a Plan A— but there was also a Plan B and a Plan C. God lets us pick. Still, I prayed *a lot* about this decision. I asked God to help me make the right choice. Of course, I picked Plan A, which was to leave home for two years and train with Bela for the Olympics. In hindsight it obviously looks like the right decision, but who's to say that Plans B and C wouldn't have been great too? If I'd chosen Plan B, you might know me today as the star of the hit medical drama *Mary Lou, M.D.* Or, I might still be living in Fairmont, enjoying the challenges of raising a family and living a much more private life.

There's an old fable about a town that was besieged by torrential rains that clearly illustrates this point. The rain poured down — not for forty days and forty nights — but for a good, long time. Long enough and hard enough for the rivers to overflow their banks and assault the town. Rescue workers labored tirelessly, day and night, seeking out and rescuing people who were about to be washed away with their homes. Among them was a man, let's call him Mark, who had always professed his great faith in God.

The rising waters had already forced Mark up to the second floor of his house, and he couldn't see how he was ever going to make it to safety. But he had faith. "I know God will deliver me," Mark repeated over and over to himself (since there was no one within earshot to hear him).

When Mark spotted a rescue boat approaching his house, he didn't move a muscle. "Jump down," the man in the boat hollered up to Mark. "I'll get you into the boat!" Mark didn't budge.

"For goodness' sake, man, hurry up!"

But Mark still wouldn't move away from his second-floor window. "I'm staying here!" he shouted back. "God will deliver me!" With so many other people still in danger, the baffled and weary rescue worker had no choice but to move on to the next house.

The water was still rising. In no time at all it would be up above Mark's head. Still he didn't panic. As he made his way up to the roof, Mark held firm in his belief that God would deliver him.

Suddenly, Mark heard a whirring in the air and he saw a helicopter coming toward him. "Hold on! Don't worry!" the pilot called out, as he lowered a rope. "Grab on tight to the rope and I'll pull you up!"

Again, Mark didn't make any effort to cooperate. "No, thanks," he yelled. "The Lord will deliver me!" As before, the rescue worker had to move on, and the helicopter flew away.

The rains continued their fierce assault. And there was Mark, clinging to the roof of his house, his strength ebbing as his house washed away from under him. In a few moments, Mark would be underwater. With his last full breath, Mark cried out to God, "Lord, I don't understand! I had faith in you. I believed that you would deliver me. How can you let me drown?"

There was a rumble in the heavens, and then God spoke to Mark. "I sent you a boat and I sent you a helicopter. What more did you want me to do?"

As Benjamin Franklin wisely observed more than two centuries ago, "God helps those who help themselves." It's still true today. Having faith doesn't mean that we can completely forgo our responsibilities and leave everything up to Him. In the story, God gave Mark the tools he needed to survive. It was up to him to decide whether or not he'd use them.

We can apply that lesson to almost every aspect of our lives. If you're driving on a busy highway, you can pray that God will keep you safe, but that doesn't mean you shouldn't check the rearview mirror when you're changing lanes or buckle your seat belt. You can ask God to help you pass your law school entrance exams with flying colors, but it will still be up to you to put in the effort and study.

The next time you are faced with a critical decision or find yourself at a crossroads in your life, remember that faith is not an excuse to avoid taking charge of your situation and using every resource within your means to uncover the appropriate solution or action. God's love for us is never in doubt. But I think it's because He loves us so much that He gave us the gift of free will so that we can make choices for ourselves—choices that, step by step, will bring us closer to the happiness He wants us to reach.

The Power of Prayer

One of the best ways to unlock the mystery of the plan that God has in store for us or to determine which direction He would like us to take is to invite Him into our day. By this I mean taking the time to have regular conversations with Him about our hopes, dreams, fears, and any tough decisions we might be facing. Prayer is an extraordinary tool that we can use to initiate an ongoing dialogue with God; it allows us to give voice to our joys and sorrows, and reaffirms our faith by establishing a connection between us and the greater power beyond our sheltered world.

Growing up in my household in West Virginia, prayer was something we did every day. That's what we were taught, and my mom worked hard to instill the habit in all of us kids. From a very young age, I was able to appreciate the tremendous benefits of prayer—even saying my prayers at bedtime allowed me to reflect on the day's activities, be reminded of all that I had to be thankful for, and drift off to sleep, comforted by knowing that the Lord's love for me was strong and everlasting. As a result, it has become an extremely important part of my life, and a wonderful means of sustaining and nurturing my faith.

In Houston, when I really began to train in

Do not pray for easy lives. Pray to be stronger men. Do not pray for tasks equal to your powers. Pray for power equal to your tasks.

PHILLIPS BROOKS

earnest for the Olympics, I not only prayed for the strength to make it through the endless workouts, and for the ability to perform all my routines, I asked Him not to let me get too homesick. *That's* the kind of thing you pray about when you're fourteen years old! But two years later, at the Summer Olympics in Los Angeles, my prayers were answered in such a miraculous way that even today it seems like a dream. I know that what I achieved that day during the final competition was the result of all my hard work and the hours upon hours of training and determination—but I also believe that my faith in God and my prayers helped all my efforts come together with remarkable results.

Still, even though my prayers helped bring me to that amazing moment where I was able to march out onto the floor of UCLA's Pauley Pavilion as a member of the United States Women's Gymnastics Team, I never prayed, "God let me win!" Nor did I ask God to let somebody else fail. All I asked was that He "please give me the strength and courage to perform my best." I also prayed that all my teammates would be blessed with the same strength and courage, and that the other athletes from around the world would remain safe and healthy over the course of the competitions. Looking back, I don't for a moment think that I won the gold medal because I had the strongest faith, or God liked my prayers the best. I am convinced, however, that my prayers helped me to remain focused on the task at hand, and also helped me perform at the peak of my abilities.

Don't think I didn't have any further need for prayer after I'd won the competition. After I won my Olympic gold medal, I prayed even *harder.* Only now I was asking Him to "please keep me steady. Don't let all this go to my head." As you can imagine, it's very easy to lose sight of who you are when you're only a teenager and are suddenly overwhelmed by instant celebrity. People seem to be pulling you in every direction at once, all of them flattering you with empty words that nonetheless *sound* convincing. You can lose your head very easily. In my case, I was blessed to have both my faith and a supportive family to keep me grounded.

Since competing in the Olympics, my life has progressed and developed in ways I never would have imagined when I was growing up in West Virginia. But through all the twists and turns along the path my life has followed to this point, prayer has consistently given me the strength I've needed to confront life's challenges. In fact, I know that no matter how wonderful the church services I attend, or how powerful a passage from the Bible might be, I couldn't sustain my faith without regular conversations with God.

What do I pray for? I pray that my children grow well and strong. I pray for the continued good health of my family. I pray for guidance in the many tasks of the day, whether it's teaching my daughter to tie her shoes or giving a motivational speech to five thousand real estate agents. I pray for the right words to comfort a friend who is in trouble. And I pray for patience, when my patience is running on empty.

I also pray about the road ahead, for the ability to cope with the sudden demands and difficulties that may enter into my day. It's a good idea for all of us to acknowledge that unforeseen events and occurrences can wreak havoc on our plans, and to prepare ourselves as best we can by praying for the peace, grace, love, patience, and wisdom that will enable us to deal with situations in a healthy, productive manner. With God's assistance, we will find that we are better able to cultivate these qualities inside ourselves. Saying a prayer for the unknown is every bit as beneficial as taking extra vitamin C during the flu season.

Recently, Shannon made the decision to leave the investment brokerage house he's worked with for many years and start his own firm. It really took a lot of courage for him to leave his familiar work environment and strike out on his own. One of the best ways I'm able to support Shannon in this new venture is to pray for him. I pray that he'll always be guided by his wisdom and integrity in the countless decisions he'll have to make. I pray that our bond will only grow stronger during the ups and downs that inevitably occur with all new endeavors, no matter how well they're planned. Of course I want his business to be an unqualified success, but I also want it to make him a happier person. So I pray that he finds the happiness that comes from doing work that he really enjoys and doing it well, and from charting his own path. And so far, I'm proud to say, he's done just that.

While I have no problem asking God for things, it's extremely important to remember that He isn't Santa Claus. God is not a genie primed to grant a thousand wishes if we say the magic words. For example, I think it's fine to pray about our finances, but I think we make a terrible mistake if our prayers on this subject come down to, "God, give me money." It's not that it isn't possible for someone in a money crunch to be blessed with sudden, just-in-the-nick-of-time cash—an unexpected gift from a relative or a sudden bull market that sends our stocks soaring. I just don't believe that the overall message of anyone's prayers should ever be "Gimme, gimme, gimme." We actually stand to gain more in the long run by praying for ways to become better stewards of the money we already have, rather than for more of it to come into our hands. Remember, prayer isn't a negotiation tactic—it's an ongoing dialogue between you and our Lord that not only reminds you of His love but through that love gives you the strength to find the best solutions to your own problems.

I believe God will always answer your questions and He will also answer your prayers, but many people think that the answers are always "yes." And that's not the case. Sometimes the answer has to be "no." It may not be what we want to hear, but if that's the answer God gives, we have to accept His wisdom. I don't believe for a moment that sometimes God doesn't hear me or that He says, "I'm not going to answer Mary Lou on this one." When I was a child, I sometimes wondered, as we all do, why God "didn't answer." Wasn't I praying the right way? Hadn't I been as good a girl as I could possibly be? Had He stopped loving me? As I matured in my faith, I came to see that all the times I thought God wasn't listening, He was actually saying "No," or "Not now, you'll have to wait." And even though this response may be in our best interest, that's often really hard for us to hear.

When God Says No

Often God's answers are not the answers we're looking for, and it's important that we arrive at a place in our faith where we are able to accept whatever response He gives us. Faith is not a means to an end—rather it's a source of sustenance and inspiration that can lift our spirits and hopes, no matter how grim things may seem. So when God doesn't answer our prayers in the way we want, we need to step back and try to see the larger picture. God sees an infinite number of factors and potential consequences that we cannot, and I believe that in His all-knowing wisdom, He will always steer us down the right path. So whenever we feel discouraged, or grumble sullenly to ourselves that God has no empathy for our needs and aspirations, we need to remind ourselves that we all have an important role to play in

Be thankful that

God's answers are wiser

than your answers.

WILLIAM
CULBERTSON

His larger plan, and that we cannot underestimate His kindness and generosity. In other words, we need to have absolute *faith* in His power and His decisions and not give in to nagging doubts. This is one of the most critical steps in finding true happiness.

Take the example of *Mary Lou's Flip-Flop Shop*, an animated children's television show which Shannon and I have spent the past seven years trying to develop as a series. We envision it as a creative movement and exercise program for young children (think *Gymboree* meets *Sesame Street*) that we've both put our hearts and souls into making a reality. And there have been so many times over the years when it's been *so* close to happening, but, for one reason or another, it just hasn't worked out. We've waited and waited. And we've prayed and prayed. But as I write this, we still haven't negotiated a satisfactory deal that will put it on the air.

As any of you who've been through a labor of love know, the ups have been exhilarating and the downs have been devastating. Maybe eventually when the show gets going, we'll see the setbacks as great blessings that helped us develop a stronger creative vision for the program that will greatly enhance its success. Maybe we just haven't met that ideal television producer who will pour his heart and soul into the show and make it a phenomenon with children everywhere. Or maybe our program will never go on the air at all. I have to believe that whatever the outcome, it's the best thing for me, and for us. Perhaps there are lessons buried here that are more valuable than any one television program. As disappointed as we've been, this humbling experience has reminded us that God will reveal only what we need to know whenever *He* decides I need to know it—and not a minute sooner.

"Thy will be done"—that's always a tough one to accept. Still, the more I've learned to surrender to God, and to have faith in His plan for me, the happier I've become. Happier, even, than if I'd received everything that I originally *thought* I wanted. Patience and humility are tremendous virtues that will only help you in your day-to-day life, and sooner or later we all have to learn to embrace these traits. Faith is a wonderful mechanism for learning to be patient and to accept our faults, fears, and failures for what they ultimately are: mere scratches on the surface of an otherwise blessed and rewarding life.

Embracing Faith Every Day

If you're already a person of faith, how often do you "take your temperature"? Do you feel disconnected from our Lord and find yourself questioning His divine love? Do you find yourself doing things from time to time that contradict your beliefs? Do you find that regularly scheduled time for your faith always slips to the bottom of the priority list? If so, perhaps it's time to take a closer look at how you've been neglecting your faith and at what efforts you can make to give it a larger place in your life. Faith is like an intricate and lovely flower garden — when nurtured and tended regularly it blooms into something glorious, but if ignored for too long, it withers and fades.

Faith is a sounder guide

than reason. Reason

can go only so far, but

faith has no limits.

BLAISE PASCAL

Once you make the firm decision to incorporate faith into your daily life, you'll find that it's much easier than you may have originally imagined. Practicing faith through disciplines such as prayer or regular church attendance becomes as natural as having three meals a day. And as your relationship with God grows deeper, and you begin to experience the

wonderful feeling of peace and fulfillment that comes from well-tended spiritual faith, you'll wonder how you ever lived without it.

Here are a few simple suggestions for ways that you can incorporate faith more easily into your daily life:

- *Enjoy prayer wherever, whenever you can.* Although it's a source of strength and happiness for me to pray with my husband and children in our home, and while it lifts my soul to pray along with others in a worship service, I know in my heart that God is not in any one setting. He is everywhere. That's why I sometimes pray silently while I'm standing in a checkout line at the grocery store or when I'm waiting to deliver a speech or even when I'm buckling my seat belt on an airplane (I bet I'm not the only one!). Any place can become a sanctuary if we make it so—whether we're riding in a car, sitting in a theater waiting for the curtain to go up, or brushing our teeth in the morning after breakfast. God doesn't mind if you practice your faith in informal settings. You'll be amazed by how these little moments of prayer can lift your spirits and bring you closer to God.

- *Create a personal prayer ritual.* One of the best ways to enjoy your faith is to truly make it your own. You don't need to limit yourself to the prayers, psalms, and proverbs that are in the Bible or your church prayer book, although they are certainly an excellent place to start. But I think that creating your own prayer, one that incorporates the people you love along with your particular needs and situation, is a terrific way to cultivate a special, very personal relationship with God. It also helps to make the daily practice of faith more enjoyable. You can change it daily; for example, you might come up with a special prayer for the Christmas season, or for your child's birthday, or on the anniversary of the death of a loved one. You might even want to write them down and start your own collection—what a keepsake to leave to your children!

What follows is my own prayer, the one I use almost every day. If you like it, I hope you'll feel free to use it yourself.

Dear Lord,

I speak this prayer to you each day. I pray that you will continue to grant me the strength and courage to realize my goals and dreams. I pray that you will help me persevere through difficult days and through those times of disappointment and rejection. I pray that you will help me be a shining example for my children and I pray that you will always embrace our family with your grace and love. I pray to you for all these things, dear Lord, because I know that you can do all things and that no plan of yours can ever fail.

- *Greet the day with God.* We often associate saying our prayers with bedtime simply because that's when we said them as children. As an adult, I've found that a morning salutation to God is a delightful, invigorating way to start the day. Rather than stumbling out of bed and feeling grumpy because you didn't get enough sleep, or worrying about the presentation you have to give at work that day, take a moment, relax, breathe, and think about what you have to be thankful for and what you hope to accomplish in the day ahead. This is an especially effective method of regularly practicing faith for those of us with families and hectic dinner hours that seem to swallow up the evening. After a long day of working or taking care of the kids, there's been more than one occasion where I've been so tired that when I bowed my head to pray, I wound up falling asleep! But by saying a prayer first thing in the morning, you don't risk neglecting it later on and start your day off on a positive, uplifting note. Try it tomorrow. Fortunately, God doesn't care what you look like in the morning . . .

* *Say grace.* Shannon and I have tried to teach the girls that thanking God for the gift of the food we eat isn't something you do only on special occasions. Aren't we equally grateful for the breakfast, lunch, and dinner we eat every day of the week? Naturally, you don't always have to say grace when you're going through the drive-through line at McDonald's, but a silent prayer of thanks seems like the least we can do to show our appreciation for the food we eat when so many people in the world have less—even if it's only a Happy Meal.

* *Pray for others, not just yourself.* There is nothing more noble than using your relationship with God to help those who are in need. There are many jarring moments day to day where we're suddenly exposed to the tragedies and sorrows that are an all-too-real part of the world we live in. I worry a lot about how my girls will deal with some of life's harsh realities, and how I can get them to understand that there are many people out there who aren't as blessed as they are. Recently, I've been using prayer as a way to make it a little easier for them, and it's a wonderful tool that we can all use to help others and give something back to the world around us. For example, when we're driving in the car and we see an ambulance, we pull over and each of says our own prayer for the person inside. As the kids grow older, I think it will help them learn to give of themselves to the people around them, and it's a beneficial exercise for all of us, no matter what age we are.

- *Share your faith with those around you.* Instead of seeing your family, friends, or professional responsibilities as competing with your faith for your limited time, try to find ways to integrate them into one activity. It's not as hard as you may think. For example, I've found a way to practice my faith that also makes it possible for me to become more involved in my children's education. Shayla and McKenna are both enrolled in a pre-kindergarten class at our neighborhood Christian school. Every Thursday, instead of just quickly dropping our kids off and leaving, all the mothers stay for a morning prayer group where we offer prayers for our own and one another's children. We call ourselves the Gatekeepers and it's a gathering that I've really come to cherish. Lately I've been praying quite a bit for Shayla, who's been expressing a lot of anxiety, particularly about being separated from me. I know it's normal at her age, but it's still agonizing to hear your child say, in a tiny, sad little voice, "Mommy, every time you leave I feel nervous." However, ever since we began Gatekeepers and I've been listening to the experiences of the other mothers, I've found that Shayla's anxiety is easier for me to understand and accept without becoming anxious myself. In fact, almost every mother has told me that she's had a similar experience herself, and that I shouldn't worry because it's just a passing phase. As I'm learning every week, sharing your faith with others is often rewarding in ways that you never imagined. Inviting friends and family to church with you on Sunday or joining an organized prayer or Bible study group can greatly enhance your faith while giving you a chance to socialize and share your religious beliefs and experiences with others.

ULTIMATELY, THE POWER OF FAITH is a mystery to everyone. I can't *prove* that bringing faith into your life will provide you with a gateway to happiness—I just know, based on my own experience, that it can brighten your life in ways you never dreamed. For as long as I've maintained my relationship with God, that gateway has remained open for me. And the profound comfort and happiness I've found on the other side are the greatest gift I've ever received.

Relationships

*Relationships . . . are an opportunity to
express love, generosity, caring, responsibility,
and growth for all concerned. The ability
to relate deeply is extremely rewarding and
offers countless opportunities for love to
be expressed.*

MICHAEL ROWLAND,
ABSOLUTE HAPPINESS

When I was growing up in West Virginia, I spent a lot of time with my grandparents on both sides of the family, listening to them tell the entertaining stories of our family's history and marveling at some of the wonderful handiwork and heirlooms that they had skillfully produced and collected over the years. Like any other part of our incredibly diverse country, West Virginia has its own distinct cultural heritage, from recipes unlike anything you've ever tasted—such as my grandmother's decadent black walnut cake, an Appalachian specialty—to adorable dolls made from corn cobs and dried apples. But the things I always loved best were the colorful patchwork quilts that my grandmothers, and their mothers before them, had stitched by hand over the years, sewing the brightly colored squares of cloth together with their amazingly intricate needlework. Quilting is a real art form in West Virginia, and almost every bed I slept in during my childhood had at least one of these beautiful works of art laid neatly at the foot of the bed.

Traditionally, a quilt is made up of dozens of individual squares of fabric, often with dramatically different colors and patterns, which when stitched together form a larger pattern that unites the varied fabrics and shapes the overall design. The relationships we share with people in our lives are a bit like the squares of cloth that make up a quilt—as completely different, or even opposite, as they may be, they all have a unique purpose and value that contributes to the larger pattern of our lives. And just as a quilt keeps us snug and warm in the middle of winter, our relationships provide us with joyful comfort, security, and love that shield and protect us in the best and worst of times.

Few things in life are more important to our happiness than establishing deep, authentic connections with other human beings. It is these connections—the relationships we'll be exploring in this chapter—that bring texture and pattern to our lives through challenging us, entertaining us, teaching us, and sharing in our triumphs, sorrows, hopes, and fears. It is often through our relationships and interactions with others that we discover who we truly are, and who we hope to be. Life's journey can be a bumpy one, and the road becomes smoother when there are other hearts and minds that will smile and shed tears right along with us. As Winnie the Pooh's friend Piglet used to say, "It's so much friendlier with two."

We've already seen that the first deep human relationship each of us has is with our families. If you were blessed with a kind and supportive family, then it was also the first opportunity you had to experience and participate in a loving relationship. Unfortunately, far too many people today are born into family situations where caring and generosity rarely play a role in the family dynamics. And the lessons they learn as they grow up are more like something from a "How Not To" book of relationships:

Lesson 1: Always Yell Louder Than the Other Person

Lesson 2: When in Doubt, Lie

Lesson 3: Only Look Out for #1

Lesson 4: Say What's on Your Mind: If They Don't
              Like It—Tough.

If any of this sounds familiar, you're not alone. Too many of us find ourselves in relationships and friendships with other people that are more destructive than constructive. It's easy to lose sight of the fact that relationships, at their most basic level, are supposed to be a source of happiness and fulfillment. Oh sure, you may hit a rough patch with your spouse now and then or find yourself getting competitive with a coworker—after all, we're all only human and few of us, no matter how hard we try, can be faultlessly good-hearted and unselfish *all* the time. The important thing is to learn to recognize the behavior that may be counterproductive to our relationships and work to make the most of the people in our lives.

Cultivating authentic interpersonal bonds based on honesty, trust, communication, and compassion is a pivotal part of creating a satisfying life. These bonds exist in many incarnations: in our romantic relationships, in our friendships, in our rapports with coworkers and professional colleagues—and in the relationships that we develop with our role models and with the people who look to us as mentors. Each type of relationship inevitably presents its own set of challenges, which we need to meet in order to make it successful; conversely, each offers a special kind of reward if we succeed in making it work. Feeling deeply, intimately connected to other individuals is one of the simplest gateways to happiness. Even better, relationships ensure that we will have someone in our lives with whom to share our profound happiness when we finally find it. As you'll no doubt discover, happiness isn't nearly as much fun if you keep it all to yourself.

Remember, we don't always have the power to choose our families, but we *can* choose our romantic partners and friends. We alone can decide which patterns and colors to weave into the fabric of our lives. And in the end, only you can determine how truly lovely your relationship quilt will be.

Romance

What counts in making a happy marriage is not so much how compatible you are, but how you deal with incompatibility.

GEORGE LEVINGER

Chances are, when most of us hear the word "relationship," we immediately think of the love and romance that we share with our romantic partners or spouses. For many of us, an unshakable romantic bond or "true love" is something we yearn for deeply, and search for fervently until we find it. It is the idea of finding our soul mate and being united with him or her forever through marriage that most shapes our vision of what our lives should and will ultimately be.

The quest to find that one special person among the millions of individuals who populate this earth can be a long and lonely one. I was blessed enough to meet my life partner, Shannon, when I was just seventeen, but I know plenty of men and women today who are still looking for Mr. or Miss Right. I also know a fair number of people who have just given up—they're tired of the dating game and have resigned themselves to the fact that they may spend the rest of their lives in superficial romantic relationships or alone. Unlike our ancestors a hundred years ago, people today don't need to marry for money or to secure a good position in society—we all have the ability to acquire those things on our own, if we work at it. In fact, some people might make the argument that marriage and "true love" that lasts for years and years are outdated notions that simply don't apply to the modern world.

I strongly disagree, and here's why: In this age of fast-paced Internet commerce and virtual reality, space shuttles and satellites that explore the cosmos, and freeze-dried food that keeps for decades, there is still one thing that we haven't been able to improve upon or manufacture in mass quantities for sale at Wal-Mart—and that's love. I'm talking about the deep, all-encompassing kind of love that you feel when you look into the eyes of a person who has just expressed, in perfect words, a feeling or belief that you have had your whole life but never thought that anyone else would understand. Or the kind of spark that makes you feel as if you've known someone for your entire life, even if you've only just met. Or the romantic punch behind a first kiss that makes your knees wobble and your heart melt. There is something amazing, something nearly indescribable, in the emotion generated between two people who connect on a soul level that we just can't find anywhere else—which is exactly why most of us keep looking for it, and why we absolutely should continue to do so.

One of my very favorite books is *Chicken Soup for the Soul* by Jack Canfield and Mark Victor Hansen, an anthology of true inspirational stories about the wondrous things that happen to everyday people like you and me. If you aren't familiar with this book, I highly recommend it. In one of the selections, Alan Cohen writes movingly of his experience with unrequited love and what it taught him about the importance of romantic relationships: "I needed to learn to open my heart and give love without requiring anything in return . . . it was not about creating a relationship with this woman. It was about deepening my relationship with myself. We believe that we are hurt when we don't receive love. But that is not what hurts us. Our pain comes when we do not give love."

We need to keep hunting for true love as much for the sake of that other person who will benefit from being loved by us as for our own. Let's face it: Some of us will find our soul mate before we graduate from high school; for others, it will take longer. But we can never give up. Along the way, we will meet and care for people who may not end up being "the one"—but that's okay. With every step, we're learning more about ourselves and growing in a direction that is leading us closer to that special love that will last the rest of our lives.

Of course the growing doesn't stop once you find that particular man or woman. As close as you may be to your spouse or the person you're dating, you'll never be the same person. And that means that you're going to disagree from time to time. Learning to work through and circumvent the little obstacles that may arise is a natural part of any long-term relationship. But the challenges are also part of what makes a lifelong commitment so rewarding. If you can continue to grow and learn together as a couple, you'll never grow tired of one another. You will find that you are constantly discovering something new and fascinating about the person you thought you knew so well. As humans, we are each of us infinitely complex, and finding someone who loves us enough to want to peel away the layers of our hearts and minds, even if it takes fifty years, is one of life's greatest gifts.

In his wonderful autobiography, *Just As I Am*, Billy Graham writes, "Ruth and I don't have a perfect marriage, but we have a great one. How can I say two things that seem so contradictory? In a perfect marriage everything is always the finest and best imaginable; like a Greek statue the proportions are exact and the finish is unblemished. Who knows any human beings like that? Ruth likes to say 'if two people agree on everything, one of them is unnecessary.' The sooner we accept that as a fact of life, the better we will be able to adjust to one another and enjoy togetherness."

One romantic union that I greatly admire is the marriage of George and Barbara Bush. I first met President and Mrs. Bush during the 1988 presidential campaign. They are fellow Houstonians and although I'd never really been involved in politics, I decided to host a prayer breakfast for the Bushes and the Quayles during the Republican National Convention. It was a wonderful experience for me because I truly believed in him and what he would do for our country. After her husband was elected, Mrs. Bush told me, "Anytime you're in Washington, give me a call and come see me for a visit."

A little while later I was in Washington for a speech, so I took her up on her offer. She invited me to come have tea with her at the White House, in the family's private living quarters. She and Millie, the Bushes' famous dog, greeted me at the private elevator going into their residence. During our visit we spoke about various things — what was happening in my life and in hers. I have a tremendous amount of respect for her. Raising five children and leading a life in the public eye is not an easy thing to do and she's done it with such grace and humility.

Over tea, she shared with me a story about her marriage to George that also appears in her book *Barbara Bush: A Memoir*. It was during the period right after her five children had all grown up and finally moved away from home and she and her husband suddenly found themselves alone together after almost twenty years. This unexpected time alone became sort of a second honeymoon for the Bushes. One day, when George came home with a cooler of redfish that he'd caught after a day of fishing, Barbara labored mightily to prepare a special dinner for the two of them. In her book, she writes, "The big moment came for our main course, and I had a dreadful time getting the smelly, slippery thing on the platter. George, not knowing I had spent hours on this project, took one look and said with a twinkle in his eye, 'You don't think I'm going to eat this . . . do you?' I burst into tears. My sense of humor had deserted me. That was almost twenty years ago, and he has raved over everything I have cooked ever since. That expression has become a password between us that always brings a giggle."

With their amazingly original array of ups and downs, romantic relationships present one of life's greatest adventures—but they are also one of life's greatest blessings. Apart from our relationship with God, the relationship that we have with our spouse is probably the most intimate we will ever know. It is worth pursuing, no matter the challenges that may stand in our way. To give romantic love, and to be loved and cherished by another, is one of the most miraculous parts of the human experience. And as such, it is a key piece of the relationship quilt and one step down our path toward happiness.

Awards become corroded, friends gather no dust.

JESSE OWENS

Friendship

The majority of the relationships in our lives will fall into the category of friendship. The term "friendship" covers a wide range of associations, from casual acquaintances and friends of friends to lifelong companions whom we've known since childhood. While friendships are not normally as intense and certainly not as intimate as our romantic relationships, they are no less rewarding. In their own way, they compel us to grow and learn more about ourselves, and to become more aware of others and their needs.

While in our romantic relationships we often define ourselves as part of a duo, especially after we are married, in friendships we are entirely on our own, accountable only for ourselves. We can't necessarily expect our friends to accept and forgive all our faults the way our spouse or the person we're dating will. My husband won't mind if I'm grumpy when I wake up the morning after I've worked late because he gets to see me all the time, and he knows that by the time he arrives home from the office I'll be in much better spirits. But if I'm in a bad mood when I have lunch with my girlfriends, whom I see only every couple of weeks because we're all so busy with our families and our careers, that's a different story! So no matter how tired I am, I'll pull myself together and put on a happy face so that we can enjoy our special time together. In this way, friends are often the people who challenge you to be the best person that you can be.

I've always tried to maintain a wide variety of friends who bring different experiences and perspectives to my life. Shannon and I don't spend time only with athletes, for example—our friends are teachers, investment bankers, journalists, and politicians. Some of them are married, some aren't; some have kids, some don't. Some we've known since our college days together, and others are more recent acquaintances. And we aren't friends with all the same people—there are plenty of people, such as the other mothers in Shayla's preschool class, whom I have become friendly with but Shannon's never met. Each one of them brings something uniquely special to my life. I can always count on my friend Erika, a wonderful cook, to brighten my day with her good-natured cheer and a fantastic quick-and-easy recipe that I can make for my family over the weekend. Or on my dear friend Angela, whose incredible serenity always calms me down just when I think I'm going to collapse from trying to manage my demanding career and be supermom all at the same time. These are just some of the many different colored fabrics that make up the friendship piece of my relationship quilt.

One particular incident that occurred during my freshman year at the University of Texas clearly showed me the importance of friendship and its lesson has stayed with me ever since. When I first enrolled at the university in 1986, I had mixed feelings about it. On the one hand, I was excited to be there. Shannon, whom I had met the previous year, was already a junior, and as the starting quarterback of the football team, a Big Man on Campus. I was looking forward to watching him play football and to leading a normal life as an undergraduate, making friends and going to parties. On the other hand, I knew it wasn't going to be easy, because my life wasn't, and had never been, *normal*. It was just two years after the Olympics and it was still impossible for me to go anywhere without being recognized and approached for an autograph or to have my picture taken with someone.

At first, I didn't see this as much of a problem, because the other students were pretty low-key around me, at least to my face. But after a while it became apparent that I was intimidating to a lot of people, and I often got the cold shoulder when I tried to make friends. Funny, huh? I'm four nine and people were afraid to approach *me*. I know now that they weren't being intentionally hurtful; they just didn't know how to deal with my celebrity, so they kept their distance. But there was one group, comprised mainly of girls, who decided from day one that they didn't like me.

As any woman knows, college-age girls can be *mean*, and these girls treated me with an attitude that bordered on cruel. They used to whisper nasty remarks behind my back, but always just loud enough for me to overhear. Then they'd be sweet as pie to my face, which made it impossible for me to call them on their behavior or defend myself. It used to hurt me so badly. I couldn't understand what I'd done to make them treat me like that. Looking back on it now, and putting myself in their shoes, I can see how they might have felt threatened by me. As teenagers do, they were working so hard to get attention and I had more than I wanted or knew what to do with.

My best friend at UT was my roommate, Laurie. Her family was originally from West Virginia and I'd met her shortly after the Olympics when I returned to attend high school in Houston. We became fast friends, and two years later, when we were both accepted at UT, we decided to room together. As it happens, she was also the one who introduced me to Shannon. But as grateful as I am to her for that, I think I'll always be most grateful for what she did to help me through the worst days of my freshman year. Laurie was a loyal and supportive friend in every way, and she was always trying to get me to laugh off those girls' biting comments and hold my head high to show them that I didn't care. But there was one night when I truly realized how much she and our friendship really meant to me.

Laurie and I and some of our other friends had gone to a party and after we'd been there awhile, I went to the bathroom. While I was still in the stall, I overheard that particular pack of girls come in and start gossiping about me. I stood there with a horrible pit in my stomach, wondering if I should try to sneak by them or remain hidden until I heard them leave. It was so awful, and I just kept thinking, "Please, God, don't let me cry." But then all of a sudden I heard Laurie's voice interject into their conversation, and, boy, did she chew them out! "Don't you guys have anything better to do than gossip about Mary

Lou? What did she ever do to you? You must be incredibly threatened by her. And you know what? I don't blame you. She's ten times the person any of you will ever be, and you know it. And that's why you spend all your energy cutting her down: to make yourselves feel better."

It's times like that when you learn who your true friends are. Laurie just went on and on, never knowing that I was hiding in there, and those girls were so stunned they couldn't even respond. At that moment I realized that the kindness and caring of one true friend were worth much more to me than the approval of a bunch of people I didn't even like. What started out as a very painful situation ended up becoming one of the nicest memories I have of my entire college experience: the moment when I realized what kind of friend I had in Laurie, and how great that knowledge made me feel.

One of the occupational hazards of being a celebrity is that many people who come into your life are not really there because of you. Michael Jordan and I talked about this once and he told me, "One thing about success that I've learned is that it changes the people around you more than it changes you. They start to look at you in a whole different frame of mind. You become a way for them to get things or accomplish things that they couldn't do in their careers."

It can be deeply trying when all the people around you are "yes" people, telling you that you're right no matter what you do, flattering you for their own interests, not yours. Famous or not, this applies to everyone. It is extremely important that each of us learn to identify the true friends in our lives and keep them close to us. For me, that's always meant my family and a relatively small number of people whom I know I can always count on. True friends are there to support you when you need it, and if they have an issue with your friendship, they'll bring it to your attention so you can discuss and resolve it.

They'll defend your character even when you aren't there (like Laurie). They'll come over to your house at midnight with ice cream after you've just broken up with your boyfriend, or bring you chicken soup and orange juice when you're sick. And they'll do these things without asking for anything in return other than your company and good conversation.

You can never have too many friends, or spend enough time with the ones you do have. As we grow older, making time for our friends becomes harder. With busy schedules and family obligations, weeks can go by without getting a chance to have lunch or coffee, or even a long leisurely phone call. We may never be able to go back to times, such as college, when we had hours to spend with our friends each day, but we still need them in our life. Even with our jobs and the responsibilities that come with raising children and looking after a home, a key part of finding happiness is to put real time and energy into your friendships. Friends are not something we can afford to let slip. And if we make it a priority, we can still find the time.

So the next time you catch yourself about to spend another evening on the sofa watching television, pick up the phone and call a friend instead. Catching up with a friend for twenty minutes is infinitely more valuable than a half hour of *Frasier*. Meals are another great venue for spending time with friends, especially for those who are perennially busy and claim they "never have time" for social obligations. You need to eat no matter what, so why not eat with a friend? Sharing a few laughs over good food will do wonders for your overall sense of well-being, and give you a chance to reconnect with someone whom you may not have seen in a while. Host a potluck supper at your house and invite all your friends and their families—you won't have to do a lot of cooking, and when everyone leaves they'll take the dishes with them! There are dozens of creative ways to make more time for the special people in your life, without infringing on your other activities or quality time with your family or spouse. The more we nurture our friendships, the greater the happiness that comes our way.

Professional Relationships

Professional relationships are inherently different from the other important relationships in our lives because we don't usually choose them in advance. There are exceptions, of course, such as if we go into business with someone we already know or if we do volunteer work with friends. But more often than not, professional relationships bring us together with people whom, under other circumstances, we wouldn't have any reason to know at all. This is both the challenge and the opportunity they present.

The most important single ingredient in the formula of success is knowing how to get along with people.

THEODORE
ROOSEVELT

It's important to realize that professional relationships are not limited to just the workplace—they can include anyone from the members of your PTA committee to the people you play softball with on Saturday. I consider professional relationships to be any relationship that is forged when you are working together with someone toward a common goal other than good times and stimulating conversation. It is this goal that brings you together initially and that shapes the dynamic of your interactions.

It's through our professional relationships that we learn about cooperation and the value of teamwork, where the need to achieve a collective goal teaches us about self-sacrifice, where we develop the capacity to rely on other people for help, and where we dig deeper into our own ability to be supportive of others. Learning to collaborate effectively with people is one of life's most important skills. When they work, these relationships are incredibly exhilarating, because they allow us to share in the sense of accomplishment that comes only from contributing to a group effort, and seeing your goals and vision through to fruition.

I am familiar with the tremendous rewards of teamwork from personal experience. Even though gymnastics is an individual sport, you're always part of a larger team and often your teammates can make or break you. Any time you compete in the compulsories and optionals you compete by team. The strongest team members go last on every apparatus, but the first members establish a scoring base that affects the later ones—kind of like the mean that sets the curve that determines the grades for a final exam. If the first one up only gets a 9.1, there's no way the last one will get a 10, even if the performance is absolutely perfect. So you depend on each other, and a strong team helps everyone individually. When I think of the word team, I think of it as an acronym—Together Everyone Achieves More.

Nevertheless, workplace relationships can be trying because often we're competing against each other for rewards and recognition, even if that's not our main intention. If we're working on a project with several other people, it's tough not to secretly hope that our boss is so impressed by our work that he or she singles us out for praise and a promotion. Similarly, it's hard not to feel resentful of a colleague who makes the same salary as we do but seems to get away with doing less work. Often professional relationships are created in an environment where we are being evaluated and measured against each other, and whether we can forge meaningful bonds with our coworkers, even amid the competition, is a terrific test of our true character.

We can make the most of our professional relationships by making a commitment to ourselves not to let our competitive side get the better of us, and to look at every situation that arises as one where teamwork is essential. One good way to do this is to focus on the larger end result of our endeavors, rather than the process and our role in it. For example, if you are working with a group of parents at your child's school to raise money for a new gymnasium, try to concentrate on the new space and how it will enhance the lives of countless young people, rather than on who among your group can pull in the largest donations. You'll find that with this attitude, your interactions with the other members of the group will improve and that your overall experience on the project will be much more pleasant and rewarding. And chances are, if you do have a boss or authority figure who is overseeing your project, he'll take notice of your positive attitude and how it kept the project moving along smoothly for everyone involved.

When handled appropriately, professional relationships can be rewarding in a very concrete way: They not only teach us to be tolerant and supportive of others and offer us a good opportunity to learn from other people's skills and knowledge but they help us accomplish specific goals that we could not have achieved on our own. It is vital that we recognize the importance of this kind of relationship, because as we travel down the road of life, we certainly can't do everything by ourselves. We need to be willing to learn from others and to graciously accept their help and advice. Professional relationships frequently open the window to new opportunities, both for the advancement of our ambitions, and the happiness that comes from working in harmony with those around us.

Mentoring

Quite often as we grow older, we become more resistant to new ideas. It's easy to understand why that happens—as our responsibilities increase, we have less time to spend learning things that don't have immediate significance in our daily lives. And we can easily fall into the trap of what I call "frozen knowledge"—when all we have to fall back on are the ideas and information that we learned in school, even though a lot of it is now outdated or no longer applicable to our current situation. As kids, we had our parents and our teachers to challenge our thinking on a daily basis, or steer us in the right direction if we were confused about a decision or problem. But who does this for us as adults?

A mentor is someone who can give us guidance and support when we are no longer in situations that are specifically geared toward learning, and a close rapport with a mentor is one of the most valuable relationships in our lives. A mentor is usually someone whom we hope to emulate, especially if we are following in their footsteps careerwise, or trying to carve out a life that's similar to theirs. While parents can and should be our most important role models, after we are grown and started down our own life path, our problems and questions may fall outside of their range of experience. I continue to seek my parents' counsel in most circumstances, but there are some instances where I need the advice of a fellow insider. After all, Dad's experience in the mining industry and my mother's experience as a housewife don't necessarily provide me with specific ways to enhance my career as a motivational speaker, or navigate the competitive world of network television as I try to secure a spot for my children's program. It's extremely important that we all find mentors who are willing to share their wealth of experience-based knowledge, and will take a genuine interest in our learning and well-being.

Often, however, we may find ourselves looking to someone we have never met as an example of what we hope to accomplish, and that's perfectly fine. As I mentioned earlier, Nadia Comaneci was my athletic role model as a child and although I eventually did get to know her and now call her my friend, many people gain inspiration and strength from people they admire from afar. If you are an aspiring writer, you probably have a favorite contemporary author or journalist whose style you admire, and with whom you'd love to chat over a cup of coffee to learn what led to his or her success. If you dabble in photography, you no doubt have a few photographers in mind whom you try to emulate and whose work is helping you to hone your own vision. As an adult, Nelson Mandela has been an important role model for me, and, I'm sure, for countless other individuals who draw strength to face their own hardships from his incredible story. A true warrior who was tested to the extreme, Mandela was willing to remain in jail for twenty-seven years in order to bring freedom to his people and reform to his country. For more than a quarter century, his faith in God and his cause never wavered and he kept up his spirits by publishing writings that would teach and bring hope to his fellow South Africans. He is a perfect example of what we can all accomplish in the face of great adversity. And even though my comfortable life is a long way from South Africa, his lessons are universal and I admire him tremendously. What an inspiration it was to watch him this past New Year's Eve as he solemnly reentered the tiny cell where he'd been held prisoner in order to light a single candle of hope for the new millennium.

Although these kinds of role models are enormously valuable, it's just as important to establish a relationship with one or more people during our lives who will advise and inspire us more directly. Doing everything on our own would be easy if we knew in advance what the outcome would be from the major decisions we need to make. Where should I go to college? Is this a good job for me? Is it smart to have another child right now? Knowing someone with more insight, wisdom, and experience is an invaluable asset when it comes to making these life-changing choices, and even some of the smaller ones. A mentor can be anyone we look up to and trust: a teacher or professor, our boss, a coworker, another adult or relative, or even one of our friends.

Throughout my life I've been blessed to meet and come to know some extraordinary people. One of them is Oprah Winfrey. I've been on her show several times and I think she's one of the most incredible women in the world. She's certainly a role model for me, as she is for millions of other women in America. She's warm and wise, and she uses her television show to bring about positive changes in people's lives through insightful discussions of current issues and events; through introducing viewers to wonderful, inspiring books; through acquainting them with impressive people; and through sharing stories of hope and courage that lift the spirits of her devotees everywhere. But I'd never thought of her as a possible mentor until one day a good friend of mine who knew how frustrated I was from bumping up against brick walls trying to get my children's show on television, casually suggested, "Why don't you call Oprah? See if she can give you some advice." I thought about it and said to myself, "Why not? I have nothing to lose."

When I called, it didn't even cross my mind that she would be available to talk to me right then. I had in mind that I would talk to her assistant, leave my name and number, and possibly set up a time in the near future for us to talk. But when I called, her assistant said, "Oh hi, Mary Lou! Oprah just got out of a meeting with her staff. Let me buzz her and see if she can take your call." At that moment I was on the cell phone in my car, pulling into the grocery store parking lot, and about to run in and buy a gallon of milk and a pack of pull-ups (the staples in our household).

Before I could even park the car, Oprah was on the line. "Hey, Mary Lou," she said. "What's up?"

I couldn't believe it had happened so quickly, and I thought to myself that if the people in the Kroger parking lot knew that I was talking to Oprah, they'd just *die*. Trying not to sound too tongue-tied, I said, "Oprah, thanks so much for taking my call. I've got a problem and I need some advice." I went on to tell her about *Mary Lou's Flip-Flop Shop* and how many times we'd come so close to having the deal done only to have it slip away in the end. "I don't know what to do," I told her, "I don't know what my next step should be."

And she was wonderful. She told me not to get discouraged because a lot of times these things take years. She gave me her inside perspective on the cutthroat television market, and advised me not to take the syndication route, because it's nearly impossible to create a loyal following for a children's show without network support. Finally, Oprah told me the most important thing I needed to hear, particularly from her: "Don't give up, Mary Lou."

When it was over, I hung up the phone and proceeded to go inside and pick up the groceries I had originally come for. That one conversation with Oprah had boosted my spirits and my confidence in a way that a hundred conversations with Shannon or my parents could never have done—because I trusted her instincts about the situation so completely. She had the insider knowledge and experience to point me in the right direction, and receiving encouragement from someone who has achieved so much in television media meant the world to me. It reaffirmed my belief in myself and the project, and made me resolve to really stick with it until the show is on the air.

Receiving guidance from our chosen mentors is only one side of the mentoring coin, and only half of a twofold opportunity to add to our relationship quilt. The other half involves becoming a mentor to someone else: a child or teenager, or a young person who is just starting out in your chosen field. This, too, can be one of the most rewarding relationships in our lives. Young people learn from us, it's true, but we can also learn from them. They remind us of what we love about our professions, of what it's like to be young and hopeful and full of dreams, and of just how satisfying it can be when our guidance and encouragement can make a difference in someone else's life.

Children will always look for role models; they're a very important part of any young person's life. But sadly in this day of instant heroes and trendy celebrities, children often find role models in the wrong places and for the wrong reasons. Ideally, a role model should be someone a child knows personally—a teacher, a relative, or a friend. Whether you think so or not, you can have a tremendous influence on the life of a child. They watch you carefully, and they see everything. Young people will learn from the way you handle situations, the way you deal with stress, your tone of voice, the way you work out problems, and the way you demonstrate the values you live by. Setting a good example is a big responsibility, but a very important one. And it's up to *all* of us—not just to the parents—to look out for future generations.

In 1996, I was privileged to be a mentor for a group of young gymnasts who were about to go through the same exhilarating but terrifying experience I had gone through twelve years earlier. It was during the summer and the Olympics in Atlanta were just a few months away, when I received a call from the United States Gymnastics Federation asking if I would come to North Carolina where the women's Olympic gymnastics team was training and give a pep talk. "You're a role model to them, Mary Lou," they told me. This particular team was very special, as many of the gymnasts had stayed and trained another four long and grueling years after Barcelona in order to have the opportunity to compete at the Games in their home country.

Feeling very honored, I immediately said yes and I boarded a plane the very next day. When I arrived, they had just finished their workout and their coach sat them down in the middle of the floor exercise mat. I was a surprise guest. When he introduced me, I walked out and saw seven pairs of eager eyes trained intently on me: Shannon Miller, Kerri Strug, Dominique Moceanu, Dominique Dawes, Amanda Borden, Jaycie Phelps, and Amy Chow—possibly the strongest team the United States would ever send to the Olympic Games.

The first question I asked was, "Is anybody scared?" Most of them answered not with words but with tears forming in their eyes. Yes, indeed they were scared. They were all aware of the pressures and expectations. They were *supposed* to bring home the team gold medal. I went on to say that it was okay to be scared, that it was completely normal. And that if any one of them *wasn't* scared, then I'd be concerned. I told them that they were ready, that they'd been preparing for this moment their entire lives. I told them that when they lined up and marched out onto the competition floor in the Georgia Dome they should hold their heads up high with complete confidence. "Be cocky," I said. "Walk into the Georgia Dome like you own it." I also told them how fortunate they were that the Olympics were going to be in their own country. I reminded them that when they heard the roar of the crowd and saw all the American flags waving, that fanfare would be for them. I urged them to enjoy every second of it, because they deserved it. I finished by saying that this was an opportunity which comes only once in a lifetime—and they should go out there and *do it!*

That team went on to win with one of the most dramatic finishes in the history of Olympic competition. They rocked the world with America's first-ever team gold medal in gymnastics. I was so proud of them. And when they were standing on the podium with those medals around their necks, watching the United States flag rise and singing our national anthem, I felt tears form in my own eyes. They *had* done it. And maybe, just maybe, in some very small way, I had helped them get there.

Even if you are already a parent with your own children to watch out for, I urge you to step outside of your immediate family and make a difference in a young person's life. Being a mentor is an incredibly fulfilling role that invites a new kind of happiness—the happiness that comes from watching someone grow to reach their full potential, and from knowing that you were able to help them in a way that other people around them could not. If you don't immediately know someone who will benefit from your wisdom and support, there are many organizations in cities around the country, such as Big Brothers and Big Sisters, who can introduce you to a young person who will greatly appreciate your attention and guidance. Or get involved with the children's program or youth group where you worship. The unique bond you share will add yet another colorful square to the wonderful quilt that you have stitched together out of the different relationships in your life.

THE SECRET TO MAKING any kind of relationship fulfilling, whether it's with your spouse or the person you're dating, your friends, your coworkers, or even with a casual acquaintance, is to communicate with one another in an effective manner. If relationships are one of the gateways to happiness, then it's safe to say that communication is the gateway to all of our relationships. Communication is the means by which the person sitting next to you at someone else's dinner table goes from being a complete stranger to, over time, a cherished friend. It's how we share our secrets, hopes, and frustrations, and how we indicate our deep love for one another. If used improperly, however, it can also be the force that generates bad feeling and drives us apart. When communication breaks down, relationships are usually quick to follow. It is only through learning to communicate in a positive and productive way that we can make the most of our myriad relationships and ensure that we never lose the people we care about due to an angry outburst or unspoken misunderstanding.

Good communication skills are easier to master than you might think. You simply need to keep a few basic principles in mind. First and foremost, good communication requires a commitment to honesty. Which doesn't mean you need to say absolutely everything that comes into your head at all times. We all have to cultivate the habit of thinking before we speak. Telling someone "You look awful today" or "Those shoes don't go with that outfit" may seem as though you're being helpful, but even if they stem from the best of intentions, hurtful words never help anyone. Honesty must always be tempered by tact and discretion, which is often what makes it such a hard rule to follow. Good communication also means knowing how to give and receive sincere praise. And above all, it requires that you learn how to really listen.

Rule # 1 : Honesty Is the _Only_ Policy

More often than not, particularly in romantic partnerships, our relationship problems stem from a lack of honesty. And they're generally not due to something as overt or deliberate as a blatant lie: "Oh, honey, that lipstick mark on my collar came from the salesgirl at Bloomingdale's who was helping me pick out the perfect shade for you." This kind of deception may get played out on the afternoon soap operas, but it rarely happens so obviously in real life. Far more often, it's not an outright lie but an absence of truth that begins to undermine true communication and, in turn, eat away at our relationships.

My husband and I have always communicated extremely well; when we were first dating, I was amazed because I felt as if I could tell him absolutely anything without the fear of being judged or misunderstood. Throughout our relationship, we've always made an effort to discuss the issues that come up with patience and candor—for example, when I was trying to decide whether or not I would become a Baptist, we had numerous hour-long discussions about what was best for me, best for our future children, best for our marriage, and best for my faith. But nevertheless, Shannon and I are only human, and occasionally we aren't completely honest with each other only because we want to avoid hurting each other's feelings or blowing things out of proportion. While our intentions may be noble, the end result of withholding the truth is never positive. In fact, withholding the truth recently caused us to come into real conflict over something that could easily have been avoided had we been more up-front and honest with each other early on, before the problem got out of hand.

Both of us work during the week, so weekends are the time when we can devote ourselves exclusively to spending time with the kids, taking care of the house, and doing all the little chores and errands that need to be done to keep things running smoothly. For a while, Shannon didn't realize that there was a problem with his thinking of the weekends as *his* free time. Oh, he'd play with the kids, and he'd do other things around the house that he felt like doing. The problem was I didn't think he felt like doing nearly enough. He'd read the paper while I was getting the kids breakfast and ready for their day. If the girls were fighting, it was Mommy who had to say, "Okay kids, break it up." It was Mommy who put the Band-Aid on the boo-boo when Shayla or McKenna scraped a knee. It was Mommy who picked up the toys. It was Mommy who got them ready for church. And it was Mommy who always had to answer the question, "What's for dinner?"

The kids could be yelling, a pot could be boiling over, the phone could be ringing, and Shannon would keep watching football. Sometimes, when we got too loud, he'd turn up the volume a bit. And often, in the midst of chaos, he would head out the door with a breezy, "Honey, I'll be right back. I'm going to Home Depot." And sometimes "right back" was more like "right back in three hours." I fumed about it under my breath, but never said anything outright, hoping that one day he'd clue in to how hard it was for me to manage everything and start helping out more.

Finally, one day after a particularly stressful Saturday morning when I didn't think I could stand it any longer, we had a "discussion" about how I was feeling. And, as discussions go, this one was pretty loud. I know that it may be hard for you to believe that little Mary Lou can yell, but I *can!* It's not my favorite voice, but I'm only human and sometimes it's the only one that comes out. I asked Shannon to consider how *he* would feel if one day I just skipped out the door for a manicure and pedicure (or even to Home Depot) and left him with the girls for an uncertain period of time. Our conversation was filled with accusations that began with needling phrases like:

"Don't you see . . ."

"How could you . . ."

"You must think . . ."

Needless to say, Shannon was upset and surprised. He was even a little hurt. "Mary Lou, if I'm not seeing something, if I'm not hearing you, you need to tell me about it. Don't keep it in. Tell me what you need me to do. Give me direction. Communicate to me what it is that you want and need from me."

All of a sudden, I felt the wind go right out of my sails. As much as I didn't want to admit it, Shannon was right. I shouldn't have assumed that he saw the chaos for what it was. I shouldn't have assumed that he perceived my stress. All too often women instinctively carry a heavier load even when their husbands can and are willing to help out. All the while the husband may simply be thinking that his wife is comfortable with the arrangement, that's she handling everything and happy to be doing it. Eventually, I came to realize that a major reason Shannon believed this was an acceptable situation was because I avoided telling him anything different. I was never honest with him about my own feelings—that I felt as if I was shouldering too much of the responsibility for running our household and that I actually needed him even *more* on the weekends.

As Shannon and I continued to talk (thankfully by this time we had moved from our "discussion" to having a real conversation), I discovered something else that surprised *me*: Shannon had been under the impression that I had more free time during the week than I actually had. He thought that because we have a nanny during the week, I was free to spend my days dealing with business matters and had plenty of time to myself to kick back and relax. But the truth is that, even with the nanny around, I end up spending most of my time with the girls. When I run errands, I take them along with me, and we still eat our meals together. Although that allows me to spend more time with them, which I love, the trade-off is that it's almost impossible for me to get any time to myself or finish all of my office work. By the time we finished talking, Shannon had a much clearer idea of how little of "my time" I had in the average week.

Why didn't I tell him sooner? Why did I let it fester? Why didn't I air my frustration before I blew my top? As I said before, Shannon and I have always communicated easily, so it wasn't as if I had any reason to believe that he wouldn't listen to me. Looking back, I think my reluctance to confront him for so long stemmed from my subconscious fear that if he didn't already understand my concerns without needing to be told, maybe it meant that he really didn't know me as well as I thought. And, if that was true, maybe he didn't love me as much either. By never expressing my feelings, I wouldn't ever have to find out if my fears had any basis in fact.

The lesson here is that even with those we love the most, those with whom we should be the most honest, we have to guard against falling into the trap of holding back the truth. Sometimes it seems easier to choke back our feelings and pretend that nothing is wrong— maybe we're too tired to have a long-drawn-out discussion, or maybe we blame ourselves for feeling dissatisfied and hope that if we just sit tight and say nothing, the situation will go away on its own. But holding back the truth can easily become a habit, and the next thing you know there's no communication. And when relationships get to that point, nobody's happy.

If I'd continued to hold in my frustration, I never would have understood that Shannon simply wasn't as aware of what was going on in the house day to day as I was. Over time, I'd developed some pretty unrealistic expectations of him. And in fact, as he pointed out, I often did the same thing to him. For example, I always expect him to deal with the family cars. There are certain things I just can't wrap my head around, and cars are one of them. I'm not aware of things like the condition of the tire treads. My ears don't pick up that little "ping" in the engine, the way Shannon's do. He knows instantly when I don't use super-unleaded gas. To me, all unleaded gas is the same and it's a big waste of money to buy the most expensive kind, but he can hear the difference in the sound of the engine. Yet I automatically expect Shannon to understand and accept the fact that I simply can't be as attentive to the car as he is.

It wasn't until our "discussion" that I realized that I was doing the same thing to Shannon with respect to child care and running the house that I felt he often did with me about my car. I always just assumed that Shannon didn't react to what was happening with the kids or to certain problems around the house because he was willfully choosing to shut them out.

It never occurred to me that his mind-set might honestly be different from mine, and that if Shannon didn't immediately jump up and turn off the stove when the pot was boiling over, it wasn't because he was deliberately ignoring it, any more than my not noticing the "ping" of the car engine was a deliberate action on my part. He just hadn't been raised—as most men aren't—to be aware that the low rumbling sound on the stove might be cause for concern. In situations like this, blame becomes pointless; it's like asking a blind person, "Can't you *see* that?"

If you can get past the "I don't believe you're not seeing this" part to where you're saying, "How can I help you see what *I* see?" it totally turns the situation around. Instead of focusing on blame, you need to encourage the other person to see things from your perspective, and have the courage to be honest about your needs and feelings. And that's what happened with us. It was a real turning point in our relationship and now he's wonderful, just wonderful. On Saturday mornings, he asks me right off, "Mary Lou, what do you need?" And guess what? I've even started to hear the difference when I forget to fill the gas tank with super-unleaded.

After that day, Shannon and I renewed our commitment to get

things off our chests sooner rather than later. We talk things through a lot more now. And we've made it a rule never to go to bed mad or even miffed with one another, following the advice of Ephesians 4:26: "Do not let the sun go down while you are still angry." If we can't reach a resolution before we go to sleep, we agree to come back to the issue the next day. The point is that if either party in a relationship, romantic or otherwise, doesn't honestly communicate what he or she needs, there's no hope for change. If you're angry with a friend because you feel she hasn't made time for you lately, address the issue in a calm but straightforward way. If you feel your boss has evaluated some of your work unfairly, make an appointment to talk it over and convey your sentiments in an honest, but pleasant and respectful manner. Being honest allows you to create the trust and move toward greater levels of understanding in your relationship. The more clearly you can communicate your feelings, and the more committed you are to addressing your own true needs and the needs of the other person, the closer you will become.

Rule # 2: Too Much Praise Is Never Enough

Sometimes problems arise in our relationships not only on account of our failure to be honest about difficult issues and feelings but from our reluctance to volunteer words of praise when things are going well. Too often we fail to communicate the good things to our spouses or, for that matter, to anybody else with whom we have a relationship. When was the last time you told someone that he or she was doing a good job? Or that you used words like: "You are such an inspiration!" "You really handled that situation well." "I'm proud of you." Or even that old standby that we discussed in Family: "I love you." The fact is that all of us need encouragement and praise on a daily basis. It lets us know that our efforts and hard work, or even just our natural patience and good humor, aren't going unnoticed by those around us. Everyone likes to be appreciated for who they are, and to feel good about themselves. At the end of the day, the fact that we have brought a little comfort or joy to someone else is what makes it all worth it.

Other than my husband and my father, the most intimate relationship I've ever had with a man was with my coach, Bela Karolyi. Not intimate in a romantic way, certainly, but in a way where he knew me better than anyone else, inside and out.

When I first decided to move to Houston, I knew there would be some very rough times. I had heard that Bela was strict, and a tough coach and disciplinarian. And he was. You knew that when you stepped inside his gym it was time to work. No goofing off; he tolerated no laziness. And as a Bela Karolyi student, you always showed up to practice—sick, tired, injured—it didn't matter. The standing joke in the gym was if you didn't show up for a workout, you were dead. (And if you weren't dead, you'd probably wish you were.)

Oh yes, there were many, many times when I didn't want to go to those workouts. Most days I was so sore all over that I could barely drag my battered little body out of bed. But I showed up anyway and gave 100 percent—no less. Because Bela expected it. That's what separated the good gymnasts from the champions. Still, there were nights when I was on the phone crying for my parents to come and get me. "I can't do this anymore," I sobbed. "The workouts are too long and too hard." (I went from a daily three-hour practice in West Virginia to two four-hour practices—more than double the time.) "He's mean. He ignores me. He's a Communist!"

In the beginning of my Olympic training, I longed for Bela's praise. He was famous for his big bear hugs: wrapping his huge arms around us tiny gymnasts. But a lot of those big bear hugs came with the whisper of "not so good" in our ears. Even if we had won a competition, Bela always saw room for improvement. He wanted perfection. And I suppose that's why he made me into an Olympic champion. But this required me to remind myself constantly that I wasn't doing what I was doing for praise—not from Bela or anyone else—but to fulfill my dream, to go for the gold. Still, those grueling days in the gym would have been just a little bit easier if every now and then, instead of finding fault, he had whispered some words of encouragement in my ears, or told me what a beautiful vault I'd done. It would have lifted my spirits considerably when I was struggling to pull myself out of bed and head to the gym.

I knew when I retired from competitive gymnastics that I would be a "praiser." And I am; I praise everyone in our family. I praise the girls for everything from staying inside the lines while they're coloring to finishing all their green beans at dinner. I know I go overboard with them sometimes, but they really do seem to be thriving. And I praise Shannon, who requires a lot of it lately because he's still nervous about his new business venture. Maybe needing praise is a hang-up that all athletes have that stems from our performance mind-set.

If I were coaching, I think more often than not what my pupils would hear from me is, "Great job! Congratulations! Let's see if we can get those scores up a little bit next time." It has always been my feeling that a positive statement followed by a suggestion or constructive criticism is a much better way of correcting mistakes. A person has a much greater chance of success if he or she is powered by confidence and enthusiasm for the task at hand, rather than trembling from fear and self-reproach. In my mind, positive reinforcement always yields the most positive results.

The most rewarding relationships we have are the ones that make us feel good about ourselves. So do whatever you can to make the people you love feel positive and optimistic about who they are and what they're doing. When your friends get a promotion, take them out to celebrate. If your sister breaks off a bad relationship, even though she may be terribly upset, tell her how proud you are of her for doing the right thing, especially since it wasn't an easy decision. Lavish your children with the praise and positive attention they need to grow up into strong, confident, and benevolent adults—even if they do something as basic as help you clear the table after dinner. You'll be amazed at how this seemingly simple philosophy can brighten your days and strengthen the bonds between you and your loved ones. Kind and generous words don't cost a thing—so don't be afraid to give them away.

Rule #3: Know When to Exercise Restraint

Quite often it's not only what we do say, but what we *don't* that's crucial to the health and longevity of our relationships. Bela was a master coach and I now know how very blessed I was to have had the opportunity to train under him. But as a fifteen- or sixteen-year-old I didn't always understand this. And as I said earlier, Bela didn't make it easy. His words were often spoken in the heat of the moment, and they could have a devastating effect on an impressionable teenage girl. For a long time, I was able to let whatever he said roll right off my back. However, even I reached my limit one day.

It was during an evening workout and we were on the uneven bars. I had been nursing a broken finger for a few weeks and bars were the most difficult event to perform. We had a very important competition coming up so I couldn't afford to take time off and rest it. Instead,

I had to work through the pain. With the upcoming meet, a national TV network sent a camera crew to film our workout and interview those of us who were going to be competing.

We started to do some of our warm-up drills—simple skills to get our rhythm and get a feel for the bars—before we began our more difficult routines. My finger was really hurting that night, but I didn't say anything or complain about it.

Unfortunately, while performing the warm-up, I completely slipped off the bar—just peeled right off—and landed on my stomach with my head cocked back. My broken finger just wouldn't allow me to hold onto the bar. I was shocked. Bela rushed over to me under the bar to make sure that I wasn't seriously hurt. Thank goodness, I wasn't—no head, back, or neck injuries. But somehow I had managed to puncture that little piece of skin that connects your lower lip to your gum. I'm not sure what it's called, but regardless, mine was gone for good.

Blood started gushing out of my mouth. Frightened and hurt (and quite honestly a little embarrassed because it was such an easy drill), I started to cry. And worst of all, the TV crew filmed every bit of it. This didn't make Bela a very happy camper.

He told me to clean up, straighten up, and get back up onto the bars. So, doing as I was told (as I always did), I went over to the chalk bowl and began rubbing some on my hands. Gymnasts use chalk on their hands to give them a better grip on the bars. But when I tried to spit on my hands (which we all did because it made the chalk stick better), blood came rushing out of my mouth again. And I lost it. I started crying even more. The sight of my own blood terrified me, and at the time I had no way of knowing that I had only a very minor injury. Bela became adamant, shouting, "Get back up on those bars!" I looked up at him thinking, "Look at me. I'm bleeding badly. What do you *want* from me?" I didn't say it aloud, but I didn't move either. And a second later, he kicked me out of the gym. He had kicked other girls out of the gym before, but never me.

Shaking with disbelief, I walked back into the locker room, and called Mr. Spiller to come and pick me up. When he arrived at the gym, my mouth and lip had started to swell, so he immediately took me to the emergency room to have it checked out. The ER doctor examined me, but said there was nothing he could do. Stitches would do no good because the skin was too delicate and besides, injuries in the mouth healed very quickly. So he gave me some anti-inflammatory tablets to help with the swelling and sent me home. Which was where I went, very upset, barely able to talk and hurting emotionally. Not only was I in pain but I had been kicked out of practice. It was all so humiliating. I was giving Bela 100 percent, but apparently that wasn't good enough.

All I wanted to do was take a hot shower and go to bed. As I was walking upstairs to my room, the phone rang. Paige answered it, and when she heard the voice on the other end, she shot me a pointed look. It was Bela. I picked up the receiver and said "Hello?" That would be the only word I would say during the whole conversation.

Bela immediately lit into me, saying, " How dare you create such a scene? I thought you were tougher than that. Don't you *ever* do that again."

I was absolutely crushed. Mary Lou, the ultimate pleaser, always looking for approval from her coach, had let him down. Tears streamed down my silent face. I hung up without saying good-bye.

I was stunned. Bela Karolyi, the king of gymnastics, had chewed me out. And for no reason as far as I could tell. I was trying my hardest. He knew my finger was injured and hurting. How *dare* he question my effort? Why would I deliberately do something to hurt or embarrass him? It was wrong of him to treat me that way after I had sacrificed so much. We were supposed to be a team. We were all going to the Olympics—*together*.

I immediately called my parents and said, "Come and get me, I'm finished." From the tone in my voice they knew that this time I was dead serious. They had always taught me to "sleep on" major decisions in order to avoid making mistakes I'd regret later. But they knew there'd be no "sleeping on it" now. Mr. Spiller was in the room during both calls. After I hung up with my folks, I looked at him and said, "Thanks for all you've done for me, but he's crossed the line. I'm going home."

I went upstairs, took a long hot shower, and packed my things. Although I didn't know it until much later, it turns out that while I was in the shower, Mr. Spiller called Bela and told him that his prize pupil, the little girl from West Virginia with all the talent, was going home. She'd finally had enough. To say the least, I didn't sleep very well that night. When 7 A.M. practice rolled around the next morning, I stayed home. And remember, you had to be dead to get away with not showing up for practice.

The morning workout finished at 11 A.M. At 11:20 A.M. the doorbell rang. It was Bela. Despite the ice bag I'd slept with all night, my mouth and face were still very swollen. He took his big hands and gently cradled my face. "Can I come in?" he asked. I mumbled a quiet "Yes."

We sat down in the Spillers' living room and Bela did something I'd never seen him do before. He apologized. "Little Body, I'm so sorry. I overreacted because I was frustrated," he said. "Please stay. I promise I'll never speak out of haste again. Please stay."

Knowing Bela, I knew what an enormous gesture it was for him to come right out and apologize, and for him to go a step farther and beg me to stay. As I thought about it, I knew that I *did* want to stay—not just for his sake but for mine. After all, I still had my dream to accomplish, and I knew that the moment I was settled back in West Virginia, I would be terribly disappointed in myself for having thrown in the towel when I was so close to reaching my goal. All because of some heated remarks. Of course in the end, I did stay and I'm certainly glad that I did. But both Bela and I learned a very important lesson from this whole experience.

Bela discovered that, at least with me, it was smarter to think before he spoke. I call this the "Count to Ten principle." When you think before you speak you prevent yourself from saying something that you'll later regret—such as wild insults that are designed to wound the other person, rather than improve your relationship. So remember, in tense situations, before you speak, you should always count slowly to the number ten. You'll find that during this brief pause, your irrational anger drains away, and you are left with a much clearer picture of the situation and of what it is going to take to resolve it. That way you can be sure to avoid saying something you may regret later.

As tempting as it may sometimes be to lash out at someone and inflict emotional pain, bringing more hurt and anger into the situation never solved anyone's problems. Too many relationships fall apart over meaningless insults flung back and forth during the heat of the moment. And once those harsh words are out there, you can't just take them back. Your goal is to make each other feel better, not worse. So take a deep breath, get ahold of your feelings, and start a constructive, honest discussion in which you can both air your grievances in a rational manner and work toward a concrete solution to the problem.

Rule #4: Be a Passionate Listener

Building strong relationships doesn't only involve thinking carefully about what we say to our friends, and using pleasant words whenever we can. There is a whole other side to the relationship equation: listening. If we don't hear what our friends are saying and try our hardest to be sensitive to the real meaning of their words, we can't engage in the effective communication that enables us to form strong ties with others and truly share in and learn from their joys and sorrows. Plus, it's safe to say that if you aren't a good listener—or better yet, a *passionate* listener—your friends will find someone else to relate their stories to.

I know that "passion" may seem like a strange word to apply to a seemingly passive activity like listening, but as you'll see in the next chapter, passion is a tool that we can always use to transform the ordinary into the extraordinary. I don't mean passion in the romantic sense, I mean passion as it relates to enthusiasm and spirit. Believe it or not, there are good and bad listeners. We've all had conversations with people who act as if they would prefer to be somewhere else— their eyes are constantly wandering around the room, or they interrupt us with off-the-subject remarks about themselves. These individuals aren't much fun to talk to. But then, there are those people who make you feel as if you are the most important person in the world and they wouldn't want to be doing anything other than listening to you. They react appropriately to what you are saying and wait until you have finished your story before they share their own. They give you a sense of truly being heard and understood, because they are passionately listening, and thinking about every word you say.

One of the best ways to strengthen your relationships is to demonstrate that you're really listening to what someone is saying to you. For instance, when a friend shares his or her news with you, rather than immediately interjecting with your own experience ("You know, that *same* thing happened to me . . ."), try to respond briefly, saying only enough to make it clear that you've been following the conversation closely ("I hear what you're saying" or "I can't believe that!"), and then go right back to listening. Or ask a relevant question about a particular detail in the story. I know that not reacting immediately to what someone is saying can be difficult; sometimes it requires a lot of self-restraint. But the other person will undoubtedly notice and appreciate how closely you are following what he or she is saying. And more than likely, you'll be the first one with whom your friend wants to share the next important piece of news.

Someone who possesses an exceptional gift for listening is First Lady Hillary Rodham Clinton. I first met her in 1995, when she presented me with the Flo Hyman Award for excellence in athletics. A year later, when I was covering the Atlanta Games for *USA Today*, I had occasion to interview both Mrs. Clinton and her daughter Chelsea for my column. Her staff told me we'd only have three or four minutes but we ended up talking for fifteen.

No matter what people may say about her husband, I really like her. She's a stoic woman, but you can see the warmth in her eyes. I'll never forget that interview, because I was struck by how attentive she was; how she was genuinely listening to everything I asked, whether or not she had been asked the same question a million times previously. She looked me right in the eye the entire time, never breaking eye contact. People who have the ability to remain completely present in a conversation are, in fact, the best communicators. And they truly bring something special to our lives.

I try to be a passionate listener, especially since, in my profession, I have the privilege of meeting and talking with an amazingly wide range of people. For instance, if I'm at a reception after one of my speeches, and people have been waiting patiently for hours just to speak with me, I always try to have at least a brief conversation with everybody. And that doesn't mean just saying, "Hi, how are ya?" over and over again. I don't ever want anyone to feel as if I'm only going through the motions of being polite, because I'm not. I genuinely enjoy meeting new people, which is probably why I've never had any difficulty in really listening to what each individual has to say.

The ability to listen—and listen attentively—is essential to the well-being of all of our relationships. When we listen, we're telling the people around us that we value them. We're telling them that we respect them. We're telling them that we care deeply about their thoughts and feelings, and that we esteem their perspective on the world. But if you still doubt the value of passionate listening, consider the following aphorism: God gave us only one mouth, but He gave us *two* ears.

LIKE SO MANY things in this life, relationships are a labor of love. They require detailed care and attention, much like the handiwork required to sew the pieces of an old-fashioned patchwork quilt together. But as you gather your loved ones around you and assemble the many different relationships that fill your life, from your romantic partner to your friends and coworkers, you'll find that they form a beautiful collage of different personalities and perspectives that will greatly enhance your happiness and well-being. Healthy relationships evoke warmth and cheer and provide us with the support and security we need day to day to meet life's challenges. It is for this reason that we should keep them close to us and make them a priority in our quest for happiness, and throughout our lives.

THE FOURTH GATEWAY

Attitude

*The greatest discovery of my generation
is that a human being can alter his life
by altering his attitude.*

WILLIAM JAMES

lthough it took him over a thousand pages to write *War and Peace,* the great Russian novelist Leo Tolstoy needed only one sentence to explain the crucial role that attitude plays in determining our happiness. He wrote, "Happiness does not depend on outward things, but on the way we see them."

Our attitude shapes the way we experience everything in the chaotic, ever-changing world around us, from a baby's cry in the early morning ("Listen to him! Thank God he's got such a healthy pair of lungs!") to the brilliant hues of the setting sun at dusk. Have you ever noticed how, on those days when you wake up in a bad mood, *everything* seems to go wrong? The bus is late, your important fax is illegible, and they're out of your favorite sandwich at the lunch counter.

And similarly, how when you bounce out of bed with a smile on your face, nothing seems to rattle you, no matter how major? You spill the milk everywhere, but it's no big deal; you get stuck in traffic but that great new song comes on the radio; and even though you're late for an important meeting, you use the situation to stay later to talk to your boss about a few new ideas you have. No matter who you are or what your circumstances, there are always two approaches to every situation: We can either focus on the negative, which doesn't get us anywhere and certainly doesn't change anything, or we can choose to embrace the positive aspects of a situation and try to turn a negative into an opportunity. It may seem like a stretch to find cause for happiness in the midst of a seemingly dire predicament—but trust me, the positive is always there. You just have to know where to look for it.

Any given situation is like a coin in that it has two distinct sides to it. Sitting on a hillside overlooking the city, Jake and Sarah are watching the sun slowly settle over the horizon. Harvest colors are streaked across the darkening sky—yellows, oranges, purples, and reds. Sarah, who has a passion for painting and art, is overwhelmed by the beauty of nature's palette. "Look at those colors!" she says excitedly. "Isn't that the most beautiful sunset you've ever seen?" But Jake looks at her in disbelief. "What's the matter with you? Don't you know what those colors *mean*? They're a result of pollutants and factory emissions that change the makeup of the atmosphere. You see those smokestacks over there?" Jake points toward three small towers in the distance. "That place should have been shut down years ago. A sunset like that probably means a second-stage health alert."

I think most of us would agree that, based on their different attitudes, Sarah is probably having a much nicer time sitting on that hillside than Jake. And I don't think any of us would be surprised to learn that Sarah is a much happier person in general. While there are always going to be difficulties and problems that we have to deal with throughout our lives, a fundamental part of being happy is knowing how to reframe a negative situation in the best way possible. The pleasure that Sarah is deriving from such a spectacular sunset is right there in front of Jake as well—he just doesn't know how to find it or grab on to it.

The problem for people like Jake is that his negative thinking is going to hold him back throughout his life. Everything is going to be twice as hard for him as it is for someone like Sarah because he's going to waste his constructive energy focusing on the obstacles and problems he encounters, rather than on positive solutions. He's going to spend so much time complaining that he overlooks many of life's most precious gifts and poisons his relationships with other people—you can bet that Sarah will think twice before she invites him along on another excursion. Worst of all, his negative "the-world-is-against-me" frame of mind is going to prevent him from seeing that his attitude is even a problem. Poor Jake doesn't see change as a possibility and, on the rare occasions that he does, it isn't something that he gets very excited about. In fact, Jake doesn't get excited or passionate about much of anything. Instead of seeing an open gateway to happiness, his cynical attitude causes him to see a tightly locked door, with bars across the windows and a barbed-wire fence running all the way around it. And he's going to spend his life feeling discouraged and miserable, when all the while happiness is right in front of him.

Attitude is something we all can control, and it's up to us which side of the happiness coin we place right side up. Any problem we encounter—a flat tire on the highway, a bug in our computer hard drive, our dog gets hit by a car—isn't made easier by a negative or pessimistic state of mind. So why not make things easier (and infinitely more enjoyable) for ourselves by cultivating and maintaining a positive outlook? The ability to find the silver lining in any cloud that comes across our path is one of the simplest keys to happiness that I know.

Like the famous Yellow Brick Road that Dorothy and her friends followed to get to the magical kingdom of Oz, I see the road leading to happiness as a path paved with glittering stones—let's call them stepping-stones—each one providing a better, healthier perspective from which to view our lives and the world around us. Each stepping-stone is a rule that we need to follow if we want to move closer to a more positive state of mind. In this chapter we'll identify six major stones along the road to the gateway of Attitude—Optimism, Confidence, Perspective, Passion, Embracing Change, and Refusing Failure—and I'll offer some practical suggestions for how you can gain solid footing on each one. By mastering each of these simple rules and applying them in your daily life, you'll find that as you begin to cultivate a better attitude, the entire world seems brighter. In fact, before long you won't even need to go looking for happiness—it will come to you.

See the Rainbow, Not the Rain

Act as if you are already happy and that will tend to make you happy.

DALE CARNEGIE

Despite what many people seem to think ("Mary Lou, are you always this perky?"), I have my share of bad days, grumpy days, and "my world has fallen to pieces" days too. However, when I do get depressed or down, I don't usually stay that way for very long. The majority of the time, I can bounce back quickly because I make a concerted effort to pull myself together and focus on the positive. The hard part is staying in that frame of mind consistently.

We all have our share of troubles; it's pretty much par for the course in this world. Sadly, many of us make the worst of the difficult situations in our lives, always thinking, "What else can go wrong?" I call this the "Other Shoe Syndrome"; you've heard one shoe hit the floor and you keep waiting for the other shoe to drop. You can't think of anything else. Well, take it from me, if that's all you're listening for, eventually you're bound to hear it. Sitting around and waiting for something bad to happen is a self-fulfilling prophecy. And it's a sure-fire recipe for unhappiness.

Over the course of my life, I've trained myself not to be worried about that other shoe. I've learned that God allows difficulties to enter my life for a reason, usually to help me grow in some way. So instead of dreading that other shoe, I look forward to it, viewing it as the "good shoe" that's coming to make clear the lesson awaiting me. The Bible tells us, "We know that in all things God works for the good of those who love him." (Romans 8:28). So in the wake of a bad experience, I watch for signs of what God may be doing, knowing that He is in control. When I see evidence of His hand at work—whether through a change in circumstances or simply in receiving encouragement from a friend—I treat that as evidence that the good shoe has now fallen. Which is how I know, you'll pardon the expression, that I'm back on solid footing again: There are no more shoes left to fall. This way, I don't waste time or mental energy anticipating another unfortunate event that may in fact never happen at all.

I'm an optimistic person by nature. All my life, the glass has always seemed half full to me, never half empty. I've been able to see what people describe as the silver lining around a dark cloud. I like to refer to it as seeing the rainbow, not the rain. Optimism is a happiness magnet. If you stay positive, good things and good people will be drawn to you. Everyone wants to be around somebody who can bring cheer and humor to any situation, and optimistic people have a way of finding good things around every corner. I've seen it happen over and over again. Unfortunately, the opposite is also true. A negative attitude is like an advertisement for unhappiness.

This is one reason why it's so important to surround yourself with positive people. It's hard enough to keep yourself in an optimistic frame of mind, so the last thing you need is someone else bringing you down. We all know someone who complains about everything, from the weather to their commute to the fact that they can't get a date. A negative attitude is like a cold—it's contagious. One person in the office starts griping about how unfair the boss is, and the next thing you know, the entire crew of employees is grumbling. When I was competing in gymnastics there was a constant pressure to perform, and perform well. My teammates and I relied on one another to stay motivated and help keep one another's spirits up. When we all felt this way, it was easy to do, but if there was even one negative person on the team, it affected everyone's morale.

That's why associating with positive-thinking people can make a world of difference in how you see things. Optimistic people feel good about themselves, and they have a knack for making others feel good too. They can help you find that rainbow if you're having trouble finding it on your own. Picking and choosing our friends and associates wisely is a very important step in cultivating optimism. But the best part is that if you are a positive person you are more likely to attract positive people who can be a wonderful influence in your life.

My positive nature seems to make people of all ages feel very comfortable coming up to me. Maybe it's also my less-than-intimidating height—with children I'm certain that's a part of it because they can talk to me directly at eye level, which they usually can't do when communicating with adults. But whatever it is, people are always stopping to chat in movie lines or the supermarket, even in public bathrooms! I've never minded (except sometimes when we're out at a restaurant trying to have a family dinner) because I've always felt it was both an honor and a responsibility to be a public figure. I see it as a challenge—and a privilege—to be able to give people inspiration and motivation in their lives. So when people tell me how much they admire my achievements—my Olympic medals, my marriage to a loving man, my two beautiful children, and my ability to balance my family life with a successful career, the visible things they know about Mary Lou Retton—I'm obviously very proud. But while I'm thankful for myself, I'm also grateful for the opportunity those conversations always give me to offer up a little encouragement. So rather than brushing people aside because I'm too busy to talk, I'll ask a young girl what she dreams about becoming when she grows up, or I'll ask the businessman who approached me in an airport to show me pictures of *his* family. It's my hope that by responding to these people positively, rather than with the abruptness of a harried celebrity, I will be able to spread some of that happiness and genuine enthusiasm out into the world. I am always extremely excited and optimistic about what the future holds for me, and I want the people whom I encounter to feel optimistic about their lives and future as well.

One very effective way to train yourself to find that rainbow is to really make an exercise out of it. The next time you are faced with a disappointing or stressful situation that you just can't wrap your head around, sit down and make a list of all the positives that you can take from the experience. You might have to think for a while, but I guarantee there is at least one. Even if your situation involves something as tragic as the death of a loved one, you might concentrate on the fact that the person's death brought you closer to some of your relatives whom you hadn't seen in years. Perhaps it inspired you to write some of the most moving and vivid poetry you've written in a long time. Or reminded you just how fleeting life really is so that you finally took the plunge and proposed to your girfriend. In every situation there is at least one lesson, and, as we've said earlier, learning is always a positive thing. Put your list somewhere where you can see it, and each time you feel the anger or bitterness creeping back, remind yourself of the rainbows you've found. There is no better way to lift your spirits. Eventually, although it may take time, you'll be able to see them without even trying.

Always Be Confident

When we know what

we have to offer and

we bring it to each

situation, that's all

we need to do.

ANNE WILSON
SCHAEF

Unshakable confidence is the basis for much of what people describe as having a "positive attitude." It's reflected in people's posture, their tone of voice, even the way they walk. By approaching the world with a firm belief in ourselves and our God-given capabilities, we suggest to others that we *expect* to succeed. And the end result is that we usually do.

Imagine that two people are up for the same position in a big company and they have identical qualifications on paper. Which one do you think has the edge? Hands down, every time, it's the one who has the most confidence, because she's able to do the best job of selling herself. I'm not talking about boasting or bragging—that will never get you very far. I'm referring to that quiet confidence in yourself that comes through loud and clear in the way you describe your qualifications, in your poise, and in the ease with

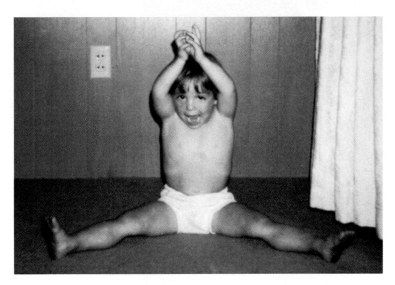

Me, at age two, attempting splits.
Courtesy of Mary Lou Retton

Sledding with my brothers and sister in West Virginia when I was three years old. I'm the one in front!
Courtesy of Mary Lou Retton

The Olympics, 1984, just after I'd stuck my vault for a perfect 10.
© *1984 by Dave Black*

Moments after sticking my vault to win the All-Around gold medal, Bela gave me one of his famous bear hugs, screaming, "We did it, we did it! You are the Olympic champion!"
© *1984 by Dave Black*

During a break at a photo shoot in the gym, Bela and I "shoot the breeze."
Courtesy of Mary Lou Retton

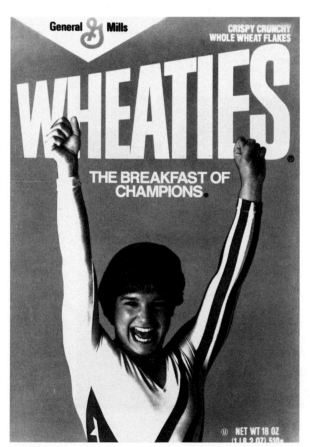

A few monthes after winning the Olympics, I found myself on the cover of the Wheaties box. At age sixteen, I was the first woman athlete to ever appear on a Wheaties box.
Photo courtesy of General Mills Inc. / Wheaties

Here I am with Shannon in 1986, one year after we met. We were at his parents' home playing Pac-Man.
Courtesy of Mary Lou Retton

Shannon and me in his college dorm in 1988.
Courtesy of Mary Lou Retton

The Retton clan on my wedding day, December 29, 1990. Left to right: Jerry, Dad, me, Mom, Shari, Donnie, and Ronnie.
Photo by Kaye Marvins

Here I am working out with some children for the Make-a-Wish Foundation. One of the girls had wished that she could "work out with Mary Lou Retton." I was so honored!
Courtesy of Mary Lou Retton

This was one of my very first corporate speeches, back in the late 1980s. What you don't see is the box I'm standing on because I'm so short!
© *Dave Black*

Shaking hands with President Gorbachev and President Ronald Reagan at a state dinner in 1986. What a thrill!
Courtesy of the Ronald Reagan Presidential Library Collection

President Reagan giving me my "one good belly laugh a day."
Courtesy of the Ronald Reagan Presidential Library Collection

THE SPORTSCENTER NEWSROOM, 10:47 A.M., AUGUST 23, 1995.

Putting a live sports news and information show on the air three times a day is never easy, and at SportsCenter there are plenty of distractions to make it even more difficult. Here, anchor Steve Levy, who's preparing for the 6:30 show, finishes his cup of coffee while Olympic Champion Mary Lou Retton works out a new routine behind him.

THIS IS SPORTSCENTER. Mornings, primetime, late night.

One of the more hilarious ESPN ads. They couldn't get rid of me!
Directed by Frank Todaro and Brian Buckley, Wieden and Kennedy

Arnold Schwarzenegger and me during our days on the President's Council on Physical Fitness and Sports.
Courtesy of Mary Lou Retton

Here I am shoving a spoonful of the "new and improved" Wheaties into Michael Jordan's mouth at a press conference in Chicago.
Photo by Charles Bennett, AP

My first meeting with Barbara Bush, a lovely and very intelligent woman.
Courtesy of the George Bush Presidential Library Collection

On the set of *Baywatch* with
David Hasselhoff and one of
the participants in *Baywatch*'s
Special Olympics.
Courtesy of Mary Lou Retton

Interviewing First Lady Hillary Rodham Clinton at the 1996 Olympics in Atlanta—the
Georgia Dome site of the Gymnastics Competition.
Photo courtesy of the White House

Three generations of Olympic champions: Nadia, Olga, and me. I keep this photo framed in my home, even today.
Courtesy of Mary Lou Retton

Here I am with the 1996 Women's Gymnastics Team at a training camp in South Carolina before they left for Atlanta. I had traveled there to give them a pep talk. What an amazing group of young women.
Courtesy of Mary Lou Retton

Me with Tipper Gore at the 1996 Olympics, cheering America's athletes on.
Callie Shell, White House

Shannon and me with the Reverend Billy Graham at his Crusade in 1999.
© *BGEA—Russ Busby*

Shannon, Shayla, McKenna, and me in our home in Houston.
Courtesy of Mary Lou Retton

Shayla and McKenna found my actual Olympic leotards and had a ball playing "nastics."
Courtesy of Mary Lou Retton

which you handle a challenging interview. When you appear confident, you gain the confidence of others, and they will view you as someone they'd like to have around. Naturally, this doesn't apply only to the job front; it's an approach that carries over into every area of your life. Confident people make better friends and spouses than people who need constant help and reassurance—no one wants to spend his or her days trying to bolster someone else's spirits and self-esteem. If you can learn to develop healthy confidence, it will propel you to new levels of success and happiness in both your personal and professional life.

There is a fine line that separates confidence from arrogance. Confidence is pleasing to others, arrogance isn't. If what you're saying makes others feel bad about themselves, or steals the spotlight away from someone else, chances are you've overstepped that line. We all know someone who likes to interject wonderful things about themselves and their accomplishments into any conversation, even if nobody's asking. Or who'll stroll right up to someone else's date and strike up a flirtatious conversation. That isn't confidence, it's merely rude and insensitive behavior. And it usually stems more from insecurity than anything else. True confidence is founded on the knowledge of God's great love for us, and it doesn't require the approval or recognition of others.

Very few of us are capable of being confident all the time. We all have moments of doubt and insecurity; I've certainly had many moments where I've questioned myself and my abilities. In truth, there were plenty of times when I thought I was crazy to think I had any chance at all of making it to the Olympics. It wasn't that I lacked confidence in my physical ability. That was almost never the case. Nor did I believe that I lacked the drive to use that ability at the highest level. But there were countless times when it seemed that no matter how

good I was, I might not have the stuff it took to beat out all the competition and make it all the way. Sometimes it kept me up at night. The
odds against me were so great—who was *I* to think I could overcome
them?

The greatest test of confidence that I've ever had occurred on a
day that started out like any other. I was training at a camp in
Louisville, Kentucky, performing with my teammates at an exhibition
under Bela's watchful supervision. The 1984 Olympic Games were
only six weeks away and I was oh so very close to achieving my dream
of making the women's gymnastics team. By this point, I'd held that
dream in my heart for so long, I couldn't remember a time when it
didn't mean everything to me.

But on that day in Louisville, it suddenly seemed that, in spite of
the years of training and hard work, fate had cruelly conspired to keep
me from realizing my dream, possibly forever. We'd finished the exhibition and I was sitting down, signing autographs. But when it was
over and I tried to stand up, I couldn't do it. My knee had locked and I
couldn't straighten it! I hobbled up to Bela and tapped him on the
hip, and said fearfully, "Bela, my knee is locked!" Bela was the ultimate practical joker, and he loved to tell funny jokes and play tricks on
people. Over the years, I had been on the receiving end of many of his
good-natured pranks. This time, he thought *I* was joking. So he looked
at me, his green eyes wide, and just laughed his deep, Bela-laugh,
"AHH, Mary Lou, now that's a good one!" And he started to walk
away, laughing and shaking his head. Of course, I wasn't joking, so I
limped after him and told him again, with nervousness in my voice,
that I could not straighten my knee. As soon as he saw that it was not a
prank, the seriousness returned to his eyes.

Panicked as I was, Bela was even more worried. But his reaction
was characteristic. He always tried to disguise his fear with anger.

"What are you doing?" he barked at me. "It's okay, it's okay," I told him, knowing it wasn't. "I'll put ice on it and it will be fine in the morning."

Somehow I made it back to my room, put a huge pack of ice on my knee, and said a prayer that what I'd told Bela would, by some miracle, turn out to be the truth. It didn't. The next morning the ice had melted, soaking the entire bed, but my knee was swollen beyond recognition. It looked as if someone had inserted a baseball where the knee used to be. I couldn't walk and Bela was still in denial, but his anger was melting like the ice and I could now see the fear in his eyes. I was crying when they took me to the hospital and I kept asking myself, over and over again, "Why me? Why now?" I just couldn't believe that with barely six weeks to go, my Olympic dream was hanging by a thread.

The hospital tests were conclusive: The knee joint had frozen up and I needed surgery. If I even tried to compete without it—which was clearly impossible—I could do permanent damage to the knee that might leave me unable to walk. Every doctor told me the same thing, that surgery wasn't debatable and all the icing down and taping up in the world couldn't change that fact. And the doctors were unanimous on this too: With a minimum of three months needed to recover from surgery, there was no way I would be ready to compete in the Olympics.

I was devastated. I had worked for almost nine years and made every imaginable sacrifice to achieve my goal. And now, six weeks before my dream was about to come true, people were telling me it couldn't happen. One doctor told me, "Just go back home to West Virginia and wait until the next Olympics."

Precisely at that moment something inside of me surged, moved, clicked, however you want to explain it, and I thought, "No one is going to tell me what I can and can't do." Nobody was going to put a limit on me. "I've made it this far!" I thought. "This is probably my only chance to compete in the Olympics and there's no way I'm going to miss it!" I summoned up all the confidence I could muster and bravely told Bela that I would have the surgery but that he could absolutely count on me to be ready.

I had the surgery and immediately began rehabilitating my knee. The very next day I was up and walking, even though my knee was sore and the nurses kept telling me to get back into bed. The following day I was jogging and by the third day after surgery I was back up on the parallel bars! My doctors were horrified and I knew that I was risking hurting my knee even more, but after two years of intensive training I was confident in my body's strength and ability to perform under intense pressure. I also knew that if I just sat idly by and didn't even give it a shot, I never would have forgiven myself. So I worked like a maniac and squeezed three months of rehabilitation into three weeks. Only Bela believed that I could do it. And that was because he knew how much I believed in myself. The whole time, I just kept telling myself, "You can do it, you can do it." No one else, not even the doctor who was monitoring my progress, thought that I would be ready to compete.

In the end, despite what everyone around me thought, I was able to make it back from the injury in time to compete in the Olympics. My confidence, my belief in myself and my physical capabilities, had been challenged like never before. But in my heart of hearts, I always knew that I was completely ready. Physically, yes, but more important, because I had worked so hard to maintain my confidence, I had never been more mentally prepared for anything in my life.

Even though my experience was unique, there's one important lesson I took away from it. I still apply it to everything I do in my life today, and it works just as effectively for me as a wife and mother as it did when I was an Olympic athlete. It's this: No matter what anybody tells you, never stop believing in yourself. It sounds so easy, yet often we're the first ones to sell ourselves short. But when your confidence remains unshakable, even in the face of people telling you that you're bound to fail, you'll eventually find a way to succeed. It may not happen right away, and it may not be in the way you originally planned—God has a way of leading us through unexpected detours—but you *will* succeed eventually. You can never go wrong by betting on yourself. I suggest you memorize Philippians 4:13 and meditate on it whenever your confidence needs to be bolstered: "I can do everything through [God] who gives me strength."

One incredibly useful tool for boosting your confidence is called "visualization." A lot of professional athletes use this technique. Visualization is the process of creating a potent mental image of something that you wish to make a reality. Conjuring up a clear vision of yourself being offered that new job you want or out on a date with someone you really like will bolster your confidence tremendously. After all, it's not too hard to feel confident about something you've already seen happening. By picturing the desired achievement or event in your mind over and over again, you're training your mind to be comfortable with the idea and giving yourself the confidence you need to go forth and turn your vision into reality.

Every day of that three-week rehabilitation period following my surgery, along with the exercises I did to strengthen my knee, I practiced visualization exercises as well. I saw myself in Los Angeles, looking up at the crowded bleachers while the public address announcer introduced me as a member of the United States Women's Gymnastics Team: "From Fairmont, West Virginia—Mary Lou Retton!" And although I can't tell you that I ever pictured a specific number on any of the judges' cards, there was one image I'd developed vividly in my mind that I carried with me all the way through to the actual day of competition. It was of me sticking a landing off the beam that caused the crowd to go wild. Every time I conjured the picture in my head, it always looked the same: My arms were stretched way up over my head and I had a smile on my face from ear to ear. So by the time I actually walked out onto the floor of Pauley Pavilion, I was exuding confidence. Not only was I absolutely certain of my ability to compete, I was confident that I would win.

Let's try a little experiment. Close your eyes, and in your mind, I want you to try and visualize an actual gateway in as much detail as possible. Maybe your gateway is a huge, gleaming structure like the Gateway Arch in St. Louis or an elaborate wrought-iron fixture like the entrance to an old English garden. Or perhaps it's just a tiny little golden gateway, like the image on the side of a McDonald's drinking cup. Once you have your gateway fixed clearly in your mind, visualize yourself standing before it and admiring it. Imagine the scene right down to the last detail: What temperature is the air around you? What color is the sky? Do you hear any noises? Then, envision yourself walking slowly through the gateway to the other side, and feel the happiness wash over you as go. Picture yourself standing on the other side, a large and lovely smile on your face, feeling completely serene in the knowledge that you have just left all your troubles and worries on the other side and a life of true happiness stretches out before you. Take a few minutes and give it a try right now.

If you simply weren't able to visualize a gateway that felt real to you, don't worry. Perhaps you were distracted. Or maybe you just thought it was silly to close your eyes in the middle of reading a book. Like any skill, visualization requires practice. It's not something you can do on the fly; you need to take your time, find a quiet space, and concentrate. But if you did see your gateway, that's great! The ability to picture something clearly, to truly see it in your mind's eye, is the first step toward building the confidence you need to turn any vision into a reality.

After my first daughter Shayla was born I gained twenty-three pounds. That may not sound like much, but remember I'm four foot nine and that's about a 25 percent increase in my entire body weight. I'd been working out every day on a stationary bike until two weeks before the baby was born and now, hard as it was for me to even think about, I had to "get back up on the horse" and lose the pounds I had gained. Immediately. Or I knew I wouldn't do it for a long time. Believe it or not, sometimes working to lose that weight felt harder than all my Olympic training, but in the end what I'd learned in my gymnastics training was what kept me going and kept my confidence up. Once again, I visualized myself succeeding. I could look in the mirror with imagination and concentration and actually see my body the way it was supposed to look—twenty-three pounds lighter—not the way it was at that moment. The strength of that image gave me the confidence I needed to stick to my diet and exercise regimen, even when it was extremely difficult. But with that slender image in my mind's eye, I knew I could do it. And that feeling of assuredness carried me through to the other side.

Keep Things in Perspective

One of the tricks to maintaining a positive attitude is to keep life's daily ups and downs in perspective. Keeping things in perspective means looking at our lives on a grand scale and reminding ourselves that today's problems are but a single, tiny bump on the vast, winding road of life. Each of our lives is like an epic novel with dozens of different chapters and story lines—old characters drop out of sight and new ones arrive to take their place; seemingly irrelevant events take on a new significance later on; some chapters are quiet and straightfoward, others are packed with melodrama; and new and interesting plot twists are the one thing you can always count on. When we actually read a book, however, we have the advantage of watching the events unfold from afar—we know what all the characters are doing and we understand their motivations. Our outside perspective enables us to make sense of things and keep forging ahead because we know that, even if we're in the midst of a truly tragic moment, we're only halfway through the book, that time will smooth over the pain, and there are situations yet to come that will make us see this event in a whole new light. In real life, it's considerably harder for us to maintain this kind of perspective. But with a little practice, we can train ourselves to remember the larger scope of our lives, just as if we're watching them from higher ground or reading about them on the pages of a book.

As an adult, the greatest test of my ability to keep things in perspective and move forward came on April 15, 1997, when I was pregnant with our second daughter, McKenna. I was in my third trimester and the baby wasn't due for three more weeks. I was in the obstetrician's office for my weekly checkup when she came in with a grim look on her face and delivered the shocking news. "You have no amniotic fluid left, Mary Lou. None." I was so stunned that I didn't immediately grasp the significance of her words, so she made them very clear. "If we don't get that baby out right now, it's very possible that she could be strangled by her own umbilical cord."

I don't know what color I turned, but I saw Shannon's face turn ashen. This was devastating news, and I wasn't sure how to handle it. I closed my eyes and prayed that God would give me and my unborn daughter the strength to get through this. "Let's go," I said, clutching my husband's hand. I didn't even have time to go home and pack a bag. They rushed me to the hospital where they immediately performed an emergency C-section.

McKenna was born with water in her lungs, taken from me—I didn't even get to hold her—and put directly into an incubator. For eight days I could only look at her tiny hands and feet, her sweet, small face through the glass pane of the incubator. I wasn't allowed to touch my own child, and my arms physically ached to hold her. Three times a day milk was pumped from my breasts and fed to her as she struggled for life.

I was unbelievably frightened and it was not the kind of fear I'd ever experienced before. When gymnastics had been the focus of my life, I'd sometimes been afraid of letting other people down if I didn't win. This was so much larger and more meaningful than any competition—and the situation was entirely out of my hands. Shannon and I sat, praying, hour after hour, hoping for a positive word from the doctors. It was one of those situations where only time would tell, and we just had to hope and pray that McKenna would be strong enough to survive. I felt as if I had been frozen in time—as if the only life I had ever known was sitting in that hospital waiting for news about my daughter. The fear was almost unbearable and I felt exhausted and sick from being so tightly wound and nervous for such a long period of time.

Even though it was a vastly different situation, I tried to draw upon the experience of my training in order to use that fear for something positive, rather than letting it paralyze me. Bela had always taught me not to get caught up in the emotion of the moment, but to keep my eye on the bigger picture. "Remember, Mary Lou," he would say, emphasizing each word with his heavy Romanian accent, "beeg picture. See it in your mind. Don't forget. Keep your eye on what's important."

So instead of curling up into a ball and withdrawing from the situation, I struggled to get outside of myself and see that bigger picture. When I finally did, I saw that my fear of losing McKenna was in reality no different than any other kind of fear I'd ever experienced. I'd never given in to my fear before and I wasn't about to start now. When I took a step back from myself, my own emotions, and the immediate experience of sitting in that waiting room terrified, I could clearly see how much Shannon and Shayla needed me to stay strong for them. Moreover, I was able to see how important it was that I remain strong for my precious little fighter, McKenna—she was going to need a resilient mother that much more because of all she was going through just to survive. I saw that this was just one challenge in the larger narrative of my life, albeit a hugely difficult one, and that no matter what the outcome was, the Lord would never give me a burden that I couldn't carry.

Finally, after eight days of agony, the doctors told us that McKenna would make it. She was taken out of the incubator and handed to me for the first time. That moment, when at last I was able to hold her, was the single happiest moment of my life. Shannon was so relieved that he doubled over crying. We had just won the most precious victory of all—the life of our daughter. Now *she* was the bigger picture: this tiny miracle I was finally holding in my arms.

The next time you feel yourself being swallowed up by a particular situation or problem—a broken heart, a crisis at work, a tiff with a friend—pause, take a deep breath, and think about where the current incident fits into the overall scheme of your life. Imagine what the "reader"—the objective observer who's been following your story since the day you were born—would tell you about how you should handle the problem. Think about the other circumstances in your life that you need to pay attention to and try to direct some of the energy you've been devoting to the current situation into them. The most important thing to remember is that, as hard as it may be, putting things in perspective can make a difficult situation much easier to bear, especially if you recognize God's ability to use everything that happens in your life. And it can help you keep up the positive attitude that will steer you down the road toward happiness.

Refuse to Believe in Failure

We all hope for a charmed life. We hope that we will be successful at whatever we do, that we will give our love to the right person, and that we will be wise enough to take advantage of every opportunity that is presented to us. But unfortunately, we are none of us perfect, and mistakes, rejection, and defeat are an inevitable part of our earthly existence. We can't always control the outcome of our actions. We can, however, control how we respond to them.

Every one of us has had experiences in life where we feel as though we've failed at something. Perhaps it was the kind of failure that can be objectively measured: You didn't pass your driving test or you didn't meet a deadline at the office. In gymnastics, the difference between winning and losing could often be measured down to a fraction of a point. With situations that have either a score or a specific target attached to them, failure is something that's clearly defined. But in most areas of life, the way we measure failure is more subtle. Usually, there's no clear definition of failure—it's only that we *feel* that we've failed in some way. If you choose to label yourself or your enterprise a failure, that's precisely what it will be. The person holding the judge's scorecard is you.

They can do all because

they think they can.

VIRGIL

I've always had a philosophical problem with the idea of "failure" because it implies that you've reached the end of an enterprise. You've given something a try and it just hasn't worked out. And you have no choice but to accept defeat and move on. But I would argue that there is no such thing as failure, that no case is ever truly closed, that no challenge is ever over. One of the easiest ways to maintain a positive attitude is to erase the word failure from your vocabulary. Just get rid of it and put it out of your mind. Learning is an ongoing process and part of learning means trying again and again until you get the results you're looking for. Sometimes you need to change your tactics or approach, but the general idea is still the same: You step back, reconsider, regroup, and give it another shot, if that's what you are inclined to do.

If you're anything like me, you're probably a very tough judge when it comes to assessing your own efforts. Despite how it may seem, even the most confident and successful people have difficulty in looking at their actions without focusing on what they perceive as their failures. Famed scientist Jonas Salk invented the polio vaccine, yet he thought he would be viewed as a failure if he didn't also discover a cure for cancer. During her tragically brief life, Princess Diana was a source of inspiration to people in hospitals around the world, often providing comfort and a sense of peace to those who were on their deathbeds. Yet we now know that she died believing that people would remember her more for the failure of her royal marriage than for any of her good works.

We all have things in our lives that we wish that we'd done differently, or situations in which we let ourselves down in some way. After the Olympics, parents across America held me up as the standard of perfection for their own children. Yet, by the age of twenty, I felt as though I'd failed them, as well as myself. I felt unqualified to be a role model. The reason, and a piece of Mary Lou Retton history that most people aren't aware of, is that I never finished college.

As I mentioned in the previous chapter, the transition to college life was very difficult for me. When I was first accepted to the University of Texas, I was thrilled. I couldn't wait to live the life of a normal teenager, meet new people, attend parties, and figure out what I was going to do with the rest of my post-gymnastics life. But when I arrived at UT I was caught off-guard by challenges I just wasn't prepared for. Not only did I have a tough time with friendships, but I also found myself struggling with the academic side because I'd been away from it for so long. During the two years I'd spent training with Bela, I didn't go to a regular high school; there just wasn't enough time in the day. Eventually, through home study and tutoring, I had received a graduate equivalency diploma or GED.

When I got to college, I assumed that my schedule would be easier, but instead, in some ways, it was fuller than ever. The media whirlwind from the Olympics continued to follow me, and I was making two or three speaking appearances a week in different cities around the country while trying to juggle a full course load. As much as I didn't want to admit it, I was trying to do too much. I just couldn't keep up with my schoolwork and even Laurie got tired of taking notes for me. It was also incredibly disorienting to be reading about the ten different ways to give a speech in a textbook, when only a day before I had given a well-received speech in front of five thousand people at one of my own speaking appearances. Or to come out of my first-year business class and go straight to a meeting with my manager and accountant in order to weigh the pros and cons of the major endorsement deals that were regularly being offered to me. In many ways I was on a completely different plane than the rest of the students, and it was a very lonely feeling. I was being pulled in two different directions by two different worlds that weren't necessarily compatible. And after a while, it just got to be too much for me—I didn't feel as if I could make the most of either opportunity, and I was tired of trying to hide my celebrity status and burgeoning public speaking career because I was afraid that the other students would resent me. After just two years, I ended up marrying Shannon and then leaving school when he graduated. I never went back.

For a long time, the fact that I didn't have a college degree was a hole inside my soul. No matter how many times I tried to convince myself that I had made the reasonable decision, I still felt that I had failed. It was worse after Shayla was born. Giving our children the best education possible has always been a priority for Shannon and me, and I absolutely intend to encourage them to go to college. But I didn't see how, when the day came for Shayla to make her own decisions about college, my opinion would have any credibility with her. As you know, one of the most important things in the world to me is being a shining role model for my children. It's something I pray for every day. Yet, in the back of my mind, I worried that my not having finished college meant that I was going to fail at that too.

Then, one day, something happened that turned my thinking completely around. I was talking on the phone with my friend Emily about an article she'd read in the newspaper about women who had gone back to college after their children were grown. In fact, many of them did it at the same time that their youngest child started as a freshman (although wisely, they were usually at different schools). One of the women had not only gotten her undergraduate degree, she had gone on to enroll in law school and was about to become a practicing attorney! It was as if someone had flipped a switch and this dark place I'd had inside me for so long, this place of embarrassment and shame, simply vanished. I suddenly realized that I'd been looking at it all wrong. Because for years now I had simply filed my lack of a college diploma as a failure, I had not even considered any other possibilities, like someday going back to school and finishing my degree. It never even occurred to me that the fact that I had started my family at such a young age meant that I would have plenty of time after the kids were grown to go back to school for six different degrees if I wanted to.

Emily had continued speaking, but I was so lost in thought that I had stopped paying attention for a moment. Suddenly, I heard her voice through the receiver. "Mary Lou? Mary Lou, are you still there? Is everything all right?"

"I'm sorry," I said. "Everything's fine. I just remembered something I have to do." Of course, being on the other end of the phone, she couldn't see the enormous smile on my face.

Today I no longer see my lack of a college degree as a failure. Of course it would have been nice to have had a normal college experience, but I've accepted the fact that it just wasn't the right time for me to be there. And I know that there's absolutely nothing standing in the way of my getting a college degree down the road. Furthermore, by going back to school as an adult, I'll have the advantage of being able to apply all my years of life experience to my studies and really make the most of my learning. Who knows, I might try something totally unexpected and daring for Mary Lou Retton, like art history or molecular biology. The possibilities are endless. The fact that I don't have a degree is no longer a failure — it's an opportunity.

Setbacks and disappointments are something we all experience at one time or another. But if you refuse to believe in failure, you'll be able to find a way to open up all those doors that at one time you thought were closed to you forever. If you mark something down as a failure, then that's what it will be. But if you make up your mind to get the better of the situation, an experience that you once labeled as a failure can become another stepping-stone toward happiness. So the next time something doesn't turn out exactly as you'd hoped, turn it around, be a fighter. Remember: It's the people who can turn a negative into a positive and bounce back who really get ahead in life.

Embrace Change

What's the scariest word in the English language? For many people, it's the word change. The idea of changing can be terrifying, even paralyzing. We all know that it's easier to cling to the familiar than to take a chance on the unknown. But as we've talked about in earlier chapters, sometimes you have to be willing to change, to leave your comfort zone, in order to find the happiness you're looking for in life. Learning to embrace change rather than avoid it is one of the key steps in developing an attitude that will enable you to achieve the happiness you seek.

Too many people remain in a bad or stagnant situation simply because they're afraid of any change. "This situation may not be ideal," we think to ourselves, "but at least I know where I stand." But unless you take the initiative to try something new, you may never know how much better things can be. Sure, change can be scary and unsettling, but it can also be challenging, exciting, and rewarding. Shaking up your life every once in a while by changing jobs, starting a new activity or hobby, or making a new friend is often the fastest way to put a little zing back into your life if you've been feeling uninspired and unfulfilled. Change is our friend, not our enemy.

Life is either a daring

adventure, or nothing.

HELEN KELLER

During the summer of 1998, I left my agent of almost nine years. It was an extremely difficult decision for me, one I agonized over for months. It was incredibly scary and painful. My agent was one of the closest people in the world to me—we talked three or four times a day, every day, and he had been involved with every aspect of my life for almost a decade. And now, suddenly, he was out of my life.

In choosing to walk away from my agent, I was definitely leaving my comfort zone. I was moving into unknown territory and it was terrifying. But I realized that I wasn't a twenty-two-year-old kid anymore; I was a thirty-year-old woman now, a wife and a mother, and I knew that I could handle whatever challenges arose. But even though a tiny insecure part of me begged me not to do it, I made the split anyway. I knew it was time. It came down to the fact that I saw a different future for myself than he did, which is what I told him. I was honest with him about what I'd been feeling for a long time. And as disappointed as he was, he understood.

For a short while I felt very alone and unsure of how to proceed. In the back of my mind, I wondered if this would mean the end of my career of giving motivational speeches, making personal appearances, and serving as a corporate spokesperson—a career that was essential to the finances of our family. I no longer had that trusted person out in the field fighting for me, representing me. Would my career vanish without him to work the phones and lobby for me? Maybe people wouldn't want to deal with me directly. Would I be able to handle the day-to-day duties of running my own office, and still devote most of my time to my children? Maybe I had made a huge mistake.

Well, those questions were answered quickly. When I became my own agent, my career flourished. My relationships with the speakers bureaus and corporations I dealt with only improved, because I was now speaking to them directly. I was able to give my input and my opinion on the theme of a speech or a script, and discuss the specific needs of each group and organization. That information was no longer coming to me secondhand, which made it easier for me to come up with the most effective speeches possible. I became available and approachable to my colleagues and they loved it—if they had a question about an airline reservation or a photo shoot they called me up and spoke directly to me. I "took the bull by the horns" as we say here in Texas, and I felt very empowered and proud. I had proved to myself that I could make my own decisions. After so many years of being managed and advised and promoted by other people, I was finally in control. And once I got over the initial shock from the change, it felt great. The best part of being in control was that when I finally decided to bring in a business manager and adviser, a wonderful man named Michael Suttle, our relationship flourished immediately because it was based on mutual respect.

One of the keys to staying positive is understanding that your life right now is not all there is to know in this world—and that change is not something to be feared—in fact it is often a harbinger of happiness. When we learn to embrace change, we open ourselves up to countless opportunities to improve our circumstances or chase the dreams that have been quiet for so long. So if you're at a point in your life where you're contemplating making a change, go for it! And if change is something that is happening to you right now—you've just ended a relationship, your youngest child has left the nest to attend college, your company just merged with another—ride it like a wave and make the most of it. Don't let your fear of the unknown prevent you from making progress on your quest for happiness.

Bring Passion to Everything You Do

Shortly after the Olympics, a reporter asked me how I had done what I did. How, she asked, did I keep going through all the pain and all the injuries? I was seventeen years old at the time and I don't know where this answer came from, but I'm very proud of it to this day. "You know," I said, "I think it's really about heart. Every great achievement is the story of a flaming heart. Every great acheivement is the result of tremendous passion."

Children possess a remarkable amount of passion. They throw themselves completely, heart and soul, into everything, whether it's building a house out of wooden blocks, or trying to get away with not eating their green beans at dinner. Children don't always know how to judge what's important and what's not, or what's realistic and what's not. At eight years old, I had a passionate dream to be in the Olympics. What was your passion as a child? Don't tell me you didn't have one, I know you did. Every little boy or girl is fascinated by dinosaurs or finger paints or wants to be a star running back in the NFL or sing on Broadway or even be elected president of the United States. Those childhood passions and dreams often sow the seeds for who we are. But sadly, most of us never try to follow our passion where it wants to take us. The mundane world of the practical takes over, and we become convinced that as grown-ups, our passionate days are over.

Rediscovering your passion and bringing it to all that you do is an absolutely essential step in cultivating the positive attitude that will lead you down the path toward happiness. Far too many of us spend our time and energy on people and projects that we just don't care about, and when that happens, the personal rewards are few and far between. In order to get more satisfaction and fulfillment out of our careers, relationships, and personal commitments, we need to reconsider how we approach them. Often this means making a change, or finding some new aspect of the person or project that will enable us to rekindle the kind of passion that will drive us to do our best. There's not much sense in devoting yourself to someone or something that you're not passionate about—it's up to us to find that passion and bring it to the fore of our activities however we can. Being passionate means giving 110 percent to any given situation; it means approaching everything in your life with that same childlike energy and enthusiasm, with an open heart and an open mind, always ready to learn, but also prepared to stumble and fall if need be. It means allowing yourself to feel deeply about whatever issues are at stake and to become personally invested in the outcome of a project or circumstance. It means turning off the "automatic pilot" that usually guides us through our daily routines, and operating from the soul.

Just as there is always some sort of positive in any negative situation, there's always something in any given situation that we can make ourselves feel passionate about. Often finding this passion involves seeing the larger picture. Even if we've been slaving away for a large investment banking firm, crunching numbers and doing research on the investment potential of an emerging industry for a boss who's anything but encouraging, we can tap into our inner passion by focusing on the personal satisfaction that we derive from doing our best, and on the millions of investors who will be able to have much more solid financial futures because of our detailed work. It's important to remember that every cog in the makeup of this vast piece of machinery we know as earth is valuable and important—I don't believe that God ever gives us a chore or a role that is unnecessary. So the next time you find yourself giving less than your best because you're bored or frustrated, remind yourself that everything we do has a larger purpose and see if you can't access some of that passion that lies inside you and channel it into your daily activities.

Sometimes, however, our circumstances are so unpleasant and difficult that there's just no way we're going to be able to make ourselves feel positive about them. If you find yourself in a situation where you absolutely cannot find a single thing to be passionate about, then it's time to reconnect with our good friend Change and strike out in search of greener pastures. Finding a way to apply your passion in any aspect of your life and finding relationships that inspire and excite you are important steps toward gaining happiness. All too often, if a brand-new goal or dream *does* come to us later in life, we believe our time for passion is past. We're set in our routine and change takes a lot of effort. We have more standing responsibilities to think about. We tell ourselves, "This is my life, this is where I've landed, and this is where I'm going to stay. Passion is kid stuff." But that's hardly the case. Passion is one of the things that makes life so worthwhile, and if you have a chance to embrace it, you absolutely should. If you can acknowledge your passion and invite it to be a regular part of your life, by changing jobs or rethinking friendships, there's no limit to the happiness you'll find.

So the next time you catch yourself going about your daily routine with a less-than-enthusiastic demeanor, think hard about whether or not you are really making the most of what life has to offer, and see if you can find any seeds of passion to bring forth into bloom. Find the child who still lives inside you and let him or her respond to your life for a day. I guarantee that when you learn to make passion a part of your everyday life, the world around you will open up to be a much brighter, much lovelier, much happier place. And that smile shining on your face won't be just the result of your newfound positive attitude—it will be the real thing, stemming from a deep-seated sense of optimism, confidence, satisfaction, and peace.

Discipline

The harder you work,
the luckier you get.

BELA KAROLYI

Even as a very young girl, I'd somehow figured out that I would have to be completely disciplined—in both body *and* mind—if I was to have any chance at all of achieving my incredibly ambitious goal of securing a spot on the U.S. Women's Gymnastics Team that would be competing at the 1984 Summer Olympic Games in Los Angeles. That meant that from the time I was eight years old, when I first began practicing gymnastics with my Olympic dream in mind, I was on some sort of schedule.

In those early years, my schedule consisted of seven hours of school followed every day by a rigorous two-hour gymnastics workout. And no matter how exhausted I was, I made myself practice every skill at least ten times, always trying to do each routine better than I had before. When I was finished with my workout, I'd do an hour of conditioning exercises and then go straight home. But my day wasn't over yet. I usually had homework and there were always chores to do around the house. By the time I crawled into bed at 9 P.M., it felt as if I'd been in constant motion since the morning. The next day, I'd get up and do it all again. And the next. And the next. For eight years my life was completely structured. It was as if I was always counting: one, two, three, four, five . . . each day following the last one in a logical sequence that would remain logical—or rational—only if I stayed focused. And that focus required discipline.

Of course, you know the rest of the story. But there's one important point to keep in mind: Even though my days were incredibly structured, and even though I focused harder on gymnastics than I had ever focused on anything in my life, nobody *forced* me to do anything. All the training, all the work—it was always my choice, right from the beginning. Discipline—the ability to marshal your energies (mental, emotional, physical) and direct them to meet the task at hand—wasn't something that was ever imposed on me. Oh sure, Bela put me through some pretty tough paces, but the decision to be there was always mine alone. In truth, I *sought* discipline, I embraced it as a loyal friend. And, throughout my life, it's rewarded that loyalty by providing me with nothing but success and happiness at every turn.

People often equate discipline with punishment, but that's a misconception. Discipline is not a dirty word. When you have discipline in your life, it's a great blessing. Believe me, I know. The world is a tough place and very few of us are capable of accomplishing our goals right away. Getting what you want out of life requires a strong sense of commitment to the hard work that will eventually enable you to achieve your dreams.

Not only is discipline a gateway to happiness in itself but it also makes it possible for us to open many of the other gateways as well. With our families, for example, we've already seen the enormous effort that's required to balance the demands of our spouse or our children with our own needs. Performing this balancing act successfully is possible only when we have the self-discipline to regularly monitor our own behavior and make sure that our priorities remain in order. For me, self-discipline often means taking the red-eye flight home when I'm working in another city so I can be home in time to get my children ready for school, and then drive them there myself. Self-discipline also means not buying that expensive toy, no matter how much my daughters might want the instant gratification (or how much I might want to play with it myself!) and, instead, investing that money in their education fund because I know it will serve them better in the long run.

As we talked about in the last two chapters, discipline is also a key part of the formula for successful relationships, as well as maintaining a positive attitude toward everything we do. It takes an extraordinary amount of self-discipline, for example, to "Count to Ten" before we say something in haste during a disagreement with a friend or co-worker. And as far as attitude is concerned, former United States Senator Bill Bradley recently summed it up when he said: "It takes discipline to be positive." He was referring to the difficulty in remaining optimistic while faced with the world's many problems, but he could just as easily have been talking about the discipline it takes for each of us to remain positive while coping with the various challenges we face throughout our lives. And the act of pursuing happiness requires tremendous mental discipline. It's that same discipline which enables us to hold the idea of that happiness firmly in our minds until we make it a reality.

Because of its importance in every aspect of our lives, learning to cultivate discipline is one of the most important steps on our journey toward happiness. Discipline consists of the skills we need to turn our dreams into more than mere hopes and fantasies—skills like preparation, perseverance, patience, and sacrifice. While maintaining discipline is never easy, there are a few sure-fire rules that can help you stay your course on the road toward your goals and ultimately become more productive, more accomplished, and more satisfied than ever before. Mastering discipline won't happen overnight, but if you apply yourself and keep these rules in mind, you'll find that discipline eventually becomes second nature. In fact, it will become almost impossible for you to approach any task that's set before you giving less than 110 percent.

Know Your Destination

Possibly the most important part of learning to develop discipline is to have a clear picture of exactly what it is we are trying to accomplish. This may sound obvious, but it's actually quite common for people to go through life drifting from one job to another and from one romantic relationship to the next without a concrete idea of what they're looking for, or what it will take to make them happy. One critical step toward happiness is figuring out what we want and need, whether it's a new job, a certain kind of car, a thriving family life, or a master's degree. The goals we set for ourselves, both short and long term, are the signposts by which we measure our progress as we journey down our life's path. They are beacons of motivation that keep us focused and moving forward; if you have established goals that are truly important to you, you're much less likely to slip into that ever-precarious comfort zone that prevents us from learning and growing.

When you're setting goals for yourself, it's extremely important that they reflect your personal values and beliefs. Take it from me—a recovering "pleaser"—it's always a bad idea to set a goal that pleases someone else before it pleases you. I'm sure that all of us are acquainted with someone who entered into a particular profession—doctor, lawyer, engineer—in order to please their parents, and who, as a result, ended up feeling frustrated and unfulfilled in their careers, even if they are considered "successful" by normal standards. And, of course, the opposite is also true. We all know people who made the decision to forgo a personal goal because their ambitions didn't sit well with somebody else. Remember, a goal isn't a real goal, and it certainly won't be a true source of motivation and satisfaction, if it isn't something you truly want and believe in. Some goals are harder to achieve than others, but trust me—the toughest ones to reach are the ones that don't have your heart behind it.

While it's essential that your goals be based on what you and you alone really want, it's equally important that they be realistic and achievable. I can already hear you saying to yourself, "Realistic? Achievable? What's *she* talking about? Isn't she the eight-year-old girl who decided that she was going to the Olympics?" Don't get me wrong. Dreams come in all shapes and sizes, and none of them are without merit. However, you do need to take into account certain practical considerations before you set your sights on any goal. Sometimes there are factors that are beyond our control. For example, if I had decided to pursue a career in *basketball* as opposed to gymnastics, I would have been—you'll pardon the expression—in over my head. There's just no way that someone who is four foot nine would ever be a great basketball player—at least not at a professional level—so it's not a very practical career goal. Similarly, if you're sixty years old and you suddenly decide that you want to be a doctor, you'll need to consider that by the time you make it through four years of medical school and three or more years of residency and on-the-job training, you'll be ready to retire. In contrast, there are many older people who find themselves going back to school for another degree simply to further their education and experience the joy of learning, and who do so with great success. So before you embark down a potentially life-altering path, take some time to think honestly about whether your goals are realistic and how the shape and structure of your life will change if you decide to pursue them. You'll find that it's considerably harder to sustain self-discipline if you're pursuing a fantasy that has absolutely no chance of ever coming to fruition.

It's also extremely important to recognize that reaching most goals requires several steps, and that achieving your goal may be a process that takes weeks or even years. Rarely do you even go from Point A, your current situation, to Point Z, your desired end result. You need to first make it to points, B, C, D, and any other stopover steps along the way. For example, there were dozens of intermediary steps between that moment on my living room floor in front of the television when I decided that I wanted to be like Nadia and my arrival at the 1984 Olympics. Not the least of these steps was signing up for my very first gymnastics class. Then there were months spent learning the basic moves, my first beginning level competitions, the regionals, nationals, and finally, years later, the invitation to move to Houston and train with Bela. Of course the idea of the Olympics always hung out there in front of me like the carrot in front of the rabbit, but in order to pace myself and avoid getting discouraged by the long process, I set smaller goals for myself along the way. At first it was just something like learning to do a back flip off the vault. But eventually it was doing my floor exercise routine absolutely perfectly for Bela in the weeks leading up to the games in Los Angeles.

For example, if you are concerned about your finances and feel that you have been living beyond your means, setting goals is the first step in taking control of your financial situation. Try to identify a practical goal, something specific and achievable. It may be that you want to purchase a home a few years from now. Perhaps you want to squirrel away money for your child's education. Or maybe you've always wanted to take a trip around the world and explore the wonders of other cultures. Your goal could even be as simple (but important) as planning a comfortable retirement for yourself, one where you won't have to scrimp and save for basics. Any one of these is the kind of goal that might motivate you to become more disciplined about money matters.

As essential as hard work and discipline are, you can't achieve any of your goals without one more thing: a *plan*. A football team relies on a play book. A builder follows a set of blueprints. They know that accomplishing their goals requires them to create and follow a solid, well-defined game plan. And the same goes for you. A plan is what allows you to map out those B, C, and D steps so that you maintain your focus and make sure that you continue to move forward toward the end result. Naturally you need to start by clearly defining your long-term goal, whatever it is. Then divide your objective down into a number of simple, short-term goals. So, if your long-term goal is to buy a new house, one of your short-term projects could be to put aside a certain amount of money into savings every week until you reach your down payment. If your long-term goal is to be a children's book illustrator, your first goal might be to sign up for some art classes and acquire the basic skills. But don't stop there. As you construct your plan, don't leave anything out. Write down even the most basic steps, such as, "research graduate programs in book illustration" or "send away for graduate school applications" or "meet with professor to discuss portfolio." The more clearly you outline the process, the easier it will be to be disciplined about moving toward your goal.

Here are four specific steps that will help you pinpoint and achieve your personal goals, no matter what they might be:

Step 1: Know What You Want. Take a moment right now to think about where you are in life, and where you want to go. Where do you see yourself a year from now? One helpful way to think about this is to jot down your thoughts in a journal or another private space where you can be completely honest without fear of being judged by others. Journal writing is also an excellent way to think about why you want to achieve this goal. If you want to lose thirty pounds because you think your boyfriend will like you better, that's not a very healthy reason for wanting to slim down. However, if you genuinely want to improve your health and appearance, and feel that you will be happier and have more energy to devote to other things if you drop a few pounds, by all means do it. The intentions behind our goals are often as important as the goals themselves—and they play a critical role in determining whether we will be able to stay disciplined and see them through to the end. Review the different areas of your life—family, relationships, work, health, finances—and identify what, if anything, you would like to achieve in this category.

Step 2: Create a Road Map. Once you've identified your goals, you can begin to devise a game plan for how best to achieve each one. Above all, *write it down*. Again, a journal can be the perfect place to construct a road map to your destination. Be as specific as possible, and do research if you have to. If you're not sure of the steps involved, seek the advice of someone who can advise you. If you're looking to move up the ladder at work, make an appointment with your boss to discuss what you need to accomplish in order to make it happen. If you're interested in applying to graduate school, make an appointment with the dean of admissions. If you're thinking about starting a retirement plan, meet with a financial adviser or a representative from your local bank. There's plenty of help available especially with fantastic resources like the Internet, if you're not sure of what your map should look like.

Step 3: Move Forward, One Step at a Time. When you've finally got it all mapped out, don't be surprised if it looks completely overwhelming. Don't let a lengthy map intimidate you. Start with the first step, and tackle it with all your heart and soul. Then, when you've accomplished step 1, move on to step 2. It may seem as if it will take an eternity to get to the end of your map, but trust me, you'll get there. Steel yourself and keep moving forward—that's what discipline is all about.

Step 4: Reward Your Successes. When you do achieve a goal (even if it's a short-term one) *reward yourself*. We're often quick to criticize ourselves when we make a mistake, but we never think to reward ourselves when we do something that turns out well. Taking pleasure in your small successes will make the process every bit as rewarding and worthwhile as the end result. As anyone knows, it's a lot easier to be disciplined when you have something to look forward to—whether it's a milk shake at your favorite ice cream parlor or that great new power lawn mower you saw at the hardware store.

Realize the Need for Sacrifice

No pain, no gain. We've all heard that expression before. Most people think of it in terms of the physical pain we endure in the course of exercising. But it's more than that. Discipline often causes pain, or at least some discomfort, because it usually means giving up something else—it means *sacrifice*. The dictionary defines sacrifice as the forfeiture of something valuable for the sake of something else. I view sacrifice as a kind of "moral investment," where what you give up now in the way of immediate gratification will eventually pay you tremendous dividends down the line. To be truly disciplined about our goals, and to keep working toward happiness at all costs, we often need to sacrifice smaller opportunities and pleasures in order to reach our end goal sooner.

Early on, I had to make a great many sacrifices in order to move myself steadily toward my goal of making the 1984 Olympic team. Some of them were small sacrifices, but some of them were pretty large and quite painful for me to make at that young age. When other kids were still playing make-believe on the playground, I was in full-scale athletic training—I was constantly doing warm-ups and workouts, and struggling to master new skills and routines. While they totally supported me and my Olympic dream, my parents certainly weren't going to let me out of my basic family responsibilities simply because I wanted to be a gymnast. I still had to help with the dishes after dinner and the laundry on the weekends. Nor were they about to let me start skipping school or neglecting my homework. It all boiled down to this: If I wanted to stay in training for the Olympics, I had to be prepared to sacrifice virtually all of my free time, all of my social time, for as long as it took. And that meant years. Of course, for a child, that was incredibly difficult. But it was my choice, and as hard as it was for me to be trapped in a netherworld between childhood and adulthood for all those years, I've never regretted making the sacrifice.

Later, when I came under Bela's demanding wing, I achieved new levels of sacrifice, even for me. Working with Bela meant getting up at ridiculously early times and practicing for hours on end, seven days a week. Being Bela's student also meant sacrificing something as simple as sleeping in on a Saturday morning to some of the more major components of a teenage girl's life such as activities with my friends, proms, and football games. And let's not forget that training under Bela had already forced me to sacrifice my home life, as well as everything that was familiar to me from my childhood. At fourteen, I found myself living with a strange family in Houston, a city almost two hundred times the size of my little hometown of Fairmont. There were times when I was so sick and tired of doing the same thing over and over and over again—one more vault, one more run-through of a floor routine, one more this, one more that—I thought I was going to *scream!* I'd start to think about all the fun I was missing and wonder what it would be like to be a normal kid, going to school every day and hanging out with friends on the weekends. But I always made myself keep going, because I knew that this degree of sacrifice was the only way I'd ever get my shot at competing in the Olympics. I never wanted to look back and think to myself, "If only I had been more disciplined in my training," or "If only I'd made one last little sacrifice."

Over the years, I've come to understand that sacrifice is actually a tremendous affirmation of faith. If sacrifice means, as it sometimes does, giving up all your comfort and all your security for something that may or may not ever come to pass, then the only certainty you have remaining is your faith. Remember *Mary Lou's Flip-Flop Shop?* As I said in the chapter on Faith, Shannon and I don't have any regrets about the sacrifices that we've made on its behalf. We've invested a lot of money that we may never see again, and we've certainly invested a lot of hours. But however it works out, the sacrifice will have been worth it because we've made it in pursuit of our dream, and we've learned some valuable lessons along the way. We continue to have faith that God will take this apparent failure and use it for something beneficial for us in the long run.

The lesson here is twofold. First, we need to realize that anything in life that's really worth achieving will probably require you to make some kind of sacrifice. That's why, as I said at the outset, I like to think of sacrifice as being an investment in the future, rather than an irreplaceable loss. Second, it takes an enormous amount of discipline to make these necessary sacrifices in life—sacrifices that may be painful at the moment, but may well prove to be the crucial turning points of your life later on. If we can accept sacrifice as a natural part of achieving our goals and working toward happiness, that discipline will come to us a lot more easily.

Don't Shy Away from Competition

When we stop to look at the world around us, it's easy to understand why competition has gotten such a bad reputation. America is a consumer culture, and it seems as if everybody is constantly trying to one-up one another by buying the hottest car or the hippest designer clothes or the biggest house on the block. Competition among people can often lead to poor behavior, coworkers gossip maliciously behind one another's backs, or two men end up slugging it out, gladiator-style, to win the affections of a woman. Frankly, it's no wonder that so many of us regard competition as something to be avoided at all costs, or that the slightest hint of a competitive atmosphere can dissuade us from pursuing opportunities and goals. But I've been a competitor all my life and after years performing in high-pressure situations, I actually believe that competition is one of life's greatest motivational gifts. When kept in proper perspective, it can really bring out the best in people. In fact, I even enjoy it.

There's no better incentive to put your best foot forward than a little healthy competition. I know from experience that I always do better when I'm competing against someone else. That was certainly the case when I left West Virginia to train with Bela. In Fairmont, I had been the big fish in our small pool of woman gymnasts, and all of a sudden, I found myself in training with girls who were not only as good as I was, some of them were much better. And do you know what? My performance actually improved dramatically because I now had a challenge, an incentive to really push myself. I desperately wanted to keep pace with these girls, and to show Bela that he hadn't made a mistake in taking me under his wing. Later on, when I was training for the Olympics, I always relied on the other girls at the gym to keep me on my toes. Sure, we called it "friendly competition," but that didn't mean we took it any less seriously. Each of us wanted to be the best. And because of that competition, we never slacked off. We didn't dare. In the end, that's what allowed each of us to reach our full potential.

In my mind, competition promotes the very best kind of discipline. It forces you to do a little more, to give a little extra. As we athletes say, it "raises the level of your game." There have been many great sports rivalries over the years that illustrate this principle: Chris Evert and Martina Navratilova in tennis; Jack Nicklaus and Arnold Palmer in golf; Magic Johnson and Larry Bird in basketball. But in the last two years, "raising the level of your game" has been redefined forever by the friendly rivalry of Mark McGwire and Sammy Sosa, whose home run competition captivated the nation. It showed all of us that we can compete to win, without ever making the other person the "enemy."

So whenever you find competition in your life—at home, at work, or even in a "friendly" game of tennis or golf—don't let yourself become intimidated and risk passing up the opportunity it brings with it. It's easy to become overwhelmed and insecure if you sense that you are out of your league.

Maybe we hesitate to apply for a job we really want because we feel intimidated by the résumé of the applicant sitting next to us. Maybe we don't try out for the basketball team because we assume that everyone will be better than us. Dropping out of the running simply because we are afraid of being shown up is the fastest way to forfeit our goals and dreams—period. We should never, ever, *not* do something simply because we are intimidated, or worried that our performance won't measure up. Instead, let the fear and competition motivate you to put forth the strongest effort you possibly can. Competition will help you cultivate the discipline that will carry you farther and faster down any road you're on. And look at it this way: If you're in a foot race toward happiness, who cares if you get there a minute sooner or a minute later than the other person? The important thing is that you are true to your goals and give your best self the chance to shine.

Stay Steady, Be Ready

You're probably familiar with the Latin phrase *carpe diem*, which translated is "seize the day." To "seize the day" means to step unflinchingly up to the plate every time an opportunity to advance your goals and dreams comes your way. Being disciplined about your ambitions and the steps you need to take to make them a reality will prepare you to seize the day every time opportunity knocks. If you've been working steadily toward your goal and are prepared to meet any challenge, you'll always be ready to grab on to success and happiness before they pass you by. And many times, those chances to grab on come when you least expect them.

Failing to prepare is

preparing to fail.

WAYNE GRETZKY

That's exactly how it was for me in 1983. I had my biggest chance to seize the moment when I least expected it. I'd gone with Bela to the American Cup, one of the biggest, most prestigious competitions in the country. But I was only at the competition as an alternate. The two girls ranked ahead of me on our team would be the ones to compete. My opportunity came when my coach came up to me the night before the competition and told me that one of the girls was injured and that I was going to compete in her place. At first I was completely shocked and taken off-guard, but then I realized that because I had been so disciplined in my training up to this point, I was prepared. I had nothing to lose, and absolutely everything to gain. In my mind, I already knew I could do it—now I just had to show everyone else.

When I competed that next morning, I drew on all those months of disciplined training and practice, and guess what? I ended up winning the title. As it turned out, it was that single event that launched my Olympic career. One little window of opportunity, as well as months of hard work in preparation for that moment, came together to give me the big break I had been waiting for.

In a perfect world there would be no such thing as pressure, but unfortunately for most of us, there's no escaping it. The good news is that if you are truly prepared, you will be ready to meet that pressure head-on. When you've been incredibly disciplined in working toward your goal and building the skills you need, the confidence you'll have as a result will give you a significant mental edge in any situation. When I was competing in the Olympics, my chance to win a gold medal came right down to the wire. In the final event, I needed to score a perfect 10 on the vault to win the gold. Everything I'd worked for my whole life was on the line. As you can imagine, the pressure was unbelievable. But as my turn grew closer, I kept reminding myself that I'd done that vault a thousand times in the gym and that I could perform it perfectly every time. The years of disciplined training allowed me to feel confident and prepared—and I was able to calm my nerves and let go of my fears. And in the end, I handled all that pressure with relative ease.

So I did my vault and scored the 10. All those years of preparation came down to a single three-second exercise. Actually, I did it twice, but because I knew in my heart that I'd already won the gold, I didn't care what happened on that second vault. It was a shining moment in time for me and I did the second one as a way of saying "thank you" to my country for having given me the opportunity to compete. At that moment, all those years of endless warm-ups and workouts, and all the inner strength I'd had to muster in order to stay focused on my goal, seemed well worth it.

Since the Olympics, I've kept up my discipline in all that I do. I continue to give 110 percent, even 220 percent, if that's what a situation calls for. And I continue to stress preparedness in my daily life, so that I am open and ready for any positive opportunities that come my way. In most cases, when I do a new product endorsement or a speaking engagement for a new company or organization, my name is enough to get me in the door the first time. But I know that if I am not totally prepared to a point where I can give these people the very best that I have to offer, there won't be a second time. When I get small parts in films or commercials, I never think, "Well, I'll just wing it, and they'll have to work with whatever they get." Instead I always do whatever it takes to be ready—from breathing exercises to going over my lines again and again.

Recently my friend Rachel found herself faced with a surprise career opportunity that she was able to jump to take advantage of simply because she had been so disciplined with her work along the way. For several years, Rachel had held an entry-level job in the editorial department of a magazine and she was anxious to move up. But while there were a number of entry-level positions at the publication, there was only one associate editor job—the position she wanted—and it was filled. Still, Rachel kept her chin up and took on a lot of extra work in addition to her normal job requirements, including some responsibilities that were normally reserved for higher level staff members. When the current associate editor decided to leave the magazine, Rachel was right there with a shining résumé that showed that she was, in essence, already doing an associate editor's job. And guess what? She got the position.

Part of developing a strong sense of discipline is doing whatever it takes to be prepared for a certain set of circumstances, even if there is no immediate opportunity on the horizon. Suppose you have a fantastic singing voice and your dream has always been to sing on Broadway, but you're a working mother with small kids at home. It's still possible, if you believe it is. Maybe the time isn't right. Maybe you'll have to wait a little bit. But you can take certain steps now, so that when your children are older, you'll be ready. Start tending to your dream by taking singing lessons. Make a demonstration tape. Do a little research at the library or on the Internet and find out if there are theatrical agents whom you can write letters to. Sometimes its hard to stay motivated when there's no immediate payoff, but you can rely on the fact that, sooner or later, your number *will* come up. And if you've been disciplined enough to keep your focus and do the relevant work in the meantime, you'll be able to leap forward and seize the day with all your might.

Manage Your Time Wisely

How many times have you heard yourself say, in a woeful tone of voice, "There just aren't enough hours in the day!"

Life would be so much easier if we could just stretch the days out like saltwater taffy and magically create more time whenever we needed it. But unfortunately, it just doesn't work that way. That's why it is so crucial to be disciplined about the time you devote to different activities. Remember, we're all working with the same amount of hours; it's what you do with those hours that makes all the difference. Peter Ueberroth, who was in charge of the 1984 Summer Olympic Games, once told his staff, "Don't work longer hours. Work *smarter* hours."

Effective time management is a discipline that requires no specific training or skill. It does require conscious effort, but the rewards, which include less stress and increased productivity, are tremendous. When you learn to take charge of your schedule and manage your commitments instead of letting them manage you, you'll discover a new sense of calm and control that spills over into every area of your life. Being disciplined about your schedule is one of the simplest ways to get a jump on your goals and make room for the truly important things in life—your family, friends, hobbies, and faith—that are so vital to your happiness and well-being. So the next time you catch yourself rushing around and feeling pressed for time, stop and check to see if you are making the most of the time you've already got.

One easy way to do it is to take an honest look at your daily routine and ask yourself this hypothetical question: If someone was willing to pay me for the time I waste every day, would I earn more money in a week than I do by working? And even though that's an attractive job description (Help Wanted: Immediate opening for couch potato; must be experienced in avoiding all forms of work), I wouldn't hold my breath. No one is ever going to make you that offer. Try to pinpoint the exact moments of the day (and we all have them) when you aren't as productive as you should be and then think about them in terms of actual minutes and hours. For example, some people spend roughly their first forty-five minutes in the office reading the paper and nursing their morning coffee before getting down to serious business. Others have trouble with that postlunch afternoon slump and it takes them an hour or so to crank back up to speed. Maybe you dawdle in the shower each morning and as a result end up skipping breakfast. Or maybe you get sucked into the evening sitcom lineup instead of doing a little extra for work, or catching up with friends on the phone.

If your answer turns out to be "yes," I'd say you've got a pretty serious time management problem on your hands. It's up to you to decide if you're ready to deal with it. But even if you answered "no," I'm sure you still recognized at least a few things that you do every day which are definitely not examples of time well spent.

There's an old expression that's usually attributed to Lucille Ball, and it goes something like this: "If you want to get a job done quickly, give it to a busy person." Lucy was right. It's the busiest people who always get more things done during their day. And there's a good reason why it works that way: It's because they've developed the discipline to cope effectively with their hectic lives. For them, one more task isn't daunting, it's hardly noticed. With focus and momentum, you can ac-complish anything.

Everybody I know has a busy life, and I'm sure that yours is no ex-ception. It's how they choose to handle that busy life that determines whether or not they ever actually get to enjoy it. The first step is to start looking at your busy life as a blessing, not a curse. The second step is to discipline yourself to become better organized. The minute you do, you'll start to accomplish more things in a single day than you'd ever thought possible. And you'll find that you don't get tired or stressed from all this new activity. Once you're really in control of your time, you'll feel more rested and relaxed during the day—even though in reality you'll actually be doing *more* than you used to. Of course the best part is that managing your time more effectively makes room for the fun things in life: leisurely walks along the beach, going for ice cream with your kids, taking a nap in a hammock, or going to a movie with friends.

Here are some of the rules I follow to organize and manage my time. Naturally you can't account for every crisis or new chore that comes along, but a few simple changes to the way you negotiate your responsibilities can make a world of difference.

- *Plan Ahead.* These days it seems like just about everyone has one of those little day planners or Filofaxes. And I have to be honest, I think they're one of the handiest tools around for us time-crunched folks. If you're serious about taking charge of your time, get one today. And map out your schedule in as much detail as possible. Think of your calendar or appointment book the way an air traffic controller thinks of his radar screen. Use it to see where things might be likely to collide in your life, and then plan ahead to prevent it. For example, if you know that you're going to be at a PTA meeting on Thursday night, try cooking a big dinner on Wednesday so that you'll have leftovers to feed yourself and your family without all the preparation and cleanup of a regular meal.

* *Prioritize.* When I have a lot of things on my plate, I don't try to deal with them all at once. I rank them in order of importance or urgency, then I tackle them one at a time. I'm a big fan of lists—during college, my apartment walls were covered with lists of assignments and due dates. Today my office, my kitchen, and even my purse are all filled with lists of pending projects, errands, and phone calls that have to be made. Prioritizing gives me a clear picture of what I need to accomplish and when, and points me in the right direction if I'm ever feeling overwhelmed. There's nothing more unproductive than spinning your wheels simply because you have so much to do you don't know where to start. Pinpoint the most important job, and dive right in.

* *Learn When to Say No.* It's never easy saying "no" to people, particularly friends or someone important like your boss. Especially if you're a "pleaser" like me, it's tough to admit that you just can't get something done. You feel like you're letting other people, and yourself, down. It takes finely tuned self-discipline to remember that you can sometimes do more harm than good when you agree to things that you might not be able to follow through on. If you're struggling with a deadline, for example, be honest with your boss and try to work toward a constructive solution or find someone else to do the job.

- *Build in Time to Rest and Relax.* We often think that it's okay to work on the weekends or during the evenings, especially if we didn't have anything else planned. But the truth is that all of us need quality time to replenish our energy. Part of effectively managing your time is learning to protect this precious time for mental and physical rejuvenation; time management doesn't ever mean working twenty-four hours a day, seven days a week. Remember, God created the universe, but even He rested on the seventh day.

Practice Patience

While you are struggling to apply yourself and build the kind of discipline we've talked about you should always keep in mind that Rome really *wasn't* built in a day. Your road to achieving your goals can be a long one, and if there's one thing that's easy to lose along the way, it's patience. Practicing patience is a form of discipline that's vitally important to anyone who is looking to find happiness. Patience is the one thing that will sustain us if that happiness isn't just around the corner, or things don't happen quite as quickly as we'd like. Most victories don't happen in seconds, or even minutes. More often it's weeks, months, and sometimes years. I always laughed when people lauded me as an overnight success. Overnight plus nine years of training, sacrifice, hard work, and discipline was more like it. But when things didn't seem to be happening quickly enough, I never allowed myself to get discouraged to the point of quitting. That's where patience was my lifesaver.

You know by now that life with Bela wasn't ever easy, and there were plenty of days when all I thought about was giving up and going home. I *loved* gymnastics—that was never in question. But coping with Bela was incredibly difficult and the Olympics seemed *so far* away. Quite frequently, I'd burst into tears on the phone with my parents and tell them I didn't think I could last another week, that it just wasn't worth it, and that they should prepare to drive down to Houston to get me. My very supportive (but also very sensible) parents would listen patiently, and then they'd always say the same thing: "Mary Lou, sleep on it. If you're still feeling the same way in the morning, we'll be right down to pick you up."

Three simple words: *Sleep on it.* What wonderful advice. Of course after a good night's rest, I woke up with renewed patience and determination toward achieving my goal. That was a big life lesson for me. And the "sleep on it" approach is a tool I still use today. No matter what the issue, whenever I'm feeling impatient or frustrated with a situation, I make myself sleep on it. I always find that it's much easier to be patient at the beginning of a new day than it is at the end of a long and very tiring one. Patience is a key part of discipline because it enables us to accept the fact that we probably won't reach our goals overnight, and to sustain our faith and a positive attitude through what might otherwise be a torturous waiting process. And you never want to risk throwing away hard work and sacrifice simply because you had to wait a little longer for the payoff.

When in Doubt, Keep Going

Well, let's say you've done everything that we've talked about so far: You've set reasonable goals for yourself, goals that define your true needs and ambitions. You've made sacrifices and been organized in your pursuit of them. You've been incredibly patient, but at the end of the day, you still don't have the results or the happiness that you want. Before you throw up your hands and ask for your money back for this book, let me tell you about the last critical component of discipline. It's called perseverance.

Perseverance means sticking to your objective and continuing to be proactive even when the going gets rough. That's what separates it from patience. It takes more than patience to keep going when there are obstacles in your path. Perseverance means seeing the obstacles for what they are, and then mapping out an alternative route, rather than sitting idly by or throwing in the towel and crawling back to your comfort zone. Perseverance is a potent combination of determination, will power, and focus that will propel you forward through any adversity.

While it's true that some people, through timing or natural talent, are instant successes, that's not usually the case. Most successful people have had their share of difficulties and failures. What sets them apart is that they didn't ever give up. You see examples of it every day, like the job applicant who gets fifty rejections, but keeps knocking on doors until she gets the perfect job. Or the struggling actor who goes out on countless auditions until he finally lands a role. Athletes work out and practice for hours on end, day after day, because they know that in order to make it to the top, they have to work at it, and work hard. There are lots of people with extraordinary natural talent who never make it. There are also lots of people with very average abilities who do. The difference is that the people in the second group have the discipline to persevere and not back down when things get difficult.

I myself certainly wasn't born with any special gift. I never had the kind of physique a gymnast is supposed to have. No long legs. No long anything. I was frequently described by the media as being built like a "fireplug." I'll leave it to you to imagine what my four older siblings were able to do with that nickname! I may not have had a classic gymnast's frame, but what I did have was the discipline to persevere through all the hardships and sacrifices which my training regimen required: no free time, lots of aches and pains, and the loneliness that stemmed from not participating in the kinds of things most other kids my age were doing. But no matter how bad it got, I kept right on going. And eventually my perseverance paid off.

All I'm saying is that it requires no unique talents or special skills to persevere. What it takes is an intense and unshakable discipline and commitment to your goal—a commitment that will focus your mind and bolster your resolve to the point where almost nothing else matters other than success.

One of the most amazing testaments to the power of perseverance in recent years is the story of Tour de France champion cyclist Lance Armstrong. Lance and I met only recently at a charity event, but before we ever met face to face, his inspiring story had already reached me and millions of others. In 1996, at the age of twenty-five, Lance was told that he had a very aggressive form of testicular cancer that had also spread to his lungs and brain. He was given only a 40 percent chance of survival. You can imagine how devastating the news was. Here he had dreamed of a phenomenal athletic career and now he was diagnosed with a serious illness that threatened to derail his ambitions before he was even out of the gate. He could very easily have given up right there. Just quit. Instead, Lance set his mind on victory. He sought out the best medical help he could find, first enduring surgery and then a painful regimen of chemotherapy. But every grueling step of the way he kept picturing himself as a winner. And that's what he was—and is. After his treatment, he was able to rehabilitate himself and get right back into competitive cycling. Lance's victory was not only over his cancer but also over the negative thoughts that told him to forgo his dream and abandon cycling. What else but the enormous power of perseverance could have enabled him to train for, enter, and win the greatest cycling competition in the world, only three years after his diagnosis? If it were a Hollywood movie (and you can bet it will be) nobody would believe it.

And as if that wasn't enough of an accomplishment for one human being in a lifetime, Lance has set up the Lance Armstrong Foundation for Testicular Cancer. He recently told the press, "If in ten years this charity raised ten million dollars a year and was able to distribute that money across the board to neurological cancers, brain cancers, breast cancers, children's cancers, then that would be an all-time career high for me." Lance Armstrong could never dream that dream were he not imbued with phenomenal perseverance.

Perseverance is the final key to developing fantastic, lasting discipline that will help you along your journey toward happiness, no matter how difficult that journey may be at times. It will help you turn

Discipline is positive.

Discipline is training.

Teaching and discipline

are inseparable.

JEAN FLEMING

your goals into real opportunities and accomplishments and cultivate a more productive, satisfying life. It has helped me to succeed time and time again, and you can put it to work in your life as well. All that's necessary is for you to decide that you want something bad enough. Then, no matter what happens along the way, perseverance will be your guide.

THE OTHER SIDE of making discipline a prominent part of your life is instilling it in others, as well as yourself. If you are a teacher, parent, or other mentor, one of the most meaningful gifts that you can give to a young person is discipline. If you love your children but don't discipline them, you aren't really following through on that love. When we discipline kids, through setting limits and boundaries, we're preparing them to become productive, happy adults. We're teaching them that their actions have consequences, and that to get ahead in life, they need to actively think about the results of behaving in a certain way and make a conscious choice whether or not that behavior is in their best interest. What more valuable gift is there?

This means that often, it's your job as a parent or guardian to tell your children what they don't want to hear:

"No, you can't ride your bike until after you finish your homework."

"If you don't eat your broccoli—all of it—there's no dessert for you."

"I bought you a video game last week. You don't need another one."

And even though you know the message has to be delivered, even though you know you've done the right thing, it can be extremely difficult to follow through on discipline when your child sulks and says, "I don't like you, Mommy!"

As the mother of two daughters who are still quite young, I don't claim to be an expert on child-rearing. I'm learning as I go and I know that I'm not perfect and neither is Shannon. But we both love our girls so much that I truly believe that any mistakes we make are the kind that won't do them any lasting harm. When it comes to our children, both Shannon and I start and finish in the exact same place: We love them more than anything else in this world. That said, I realized early on that I had to be tremendously disciplined myself in my role as a mother in order to provide Shayla and McKenna with the discipline I know they need from me. It's true that discipline is often harder on the parent than it is on the child. Discipline is a very effective form of tough love, but it's tough on you too.

Recently, I've had to deal with some disciplinary issues in regard to my four-and-a-half-year-old, Shayla. She's at that stage where's she's been getting a little sassy. You parents out there know *exactly* what I'm talking about. And it's been a bit trying for me at times. It's so tempting to just give in to her, and I've really had to steel myself in order to deal with her behavior in a way that I know is right.

One day not too long ago, we were at our local Chuck E. Cheese restaurant here in Houston. If you're not a parent, you might be unfamiliar with these establishments, but for young children they represent the fast-food equivalent of paradise. In addition to pizza and soda, they feature arcade games, prizes, and lots of noise! All of the games take tokens instead of quarters, which is probably why it's so easy to lose track of how much you're spending. That day both the girls were running through a steady stream of these tokens as if they were nothing. All they kept saying was, "Give us more, Mommy. Give us more!" Sound familiar? And when I finally said it was time to leave, Shayla pitched a terrific fit: "No! I don't want to go!" She fussed all the way from the restaurant to the car and continued her tantrum on the way home. For the first time ever, I had to pull the car over and take her out and scold her. I was shaking, I was so upset. Of course, McKenna was watching the entire scene.

I don't even know if Shayla understood what I was angry about. She's only four and a half, but her behavior was something that I just wasn't going to tolerate, not at any age. Don't get me wrong, Shayla is a very sweet, very loving little girl. Just last week, on her very first report card, she got perfect marks for her good behavior in school. Shannon and I were so proud! But the Chuck E. Cheese incident still troubles me. When I was growing up, all five of us—my brothers, my sister, and me—knew that we'd always have food on the table and clothes on our backs even if it wasn't gourmet food or designer clothes. I know that my own children are going to grow up with more than I ever had and for that I am very grateful. That day, I tried to explain to Shayla how fortunate she is, because some little boys and girls don't even get to go to Chuck E. Cheese, let alone have five dollars' worth of tokens to play with. But it's still a hard concept for a child to grasp.

This is something that I'm constantly struggling with as a mom. Yes, you want your children to have more clothes, toys, and opportunities than you did. But you don't want to spoil them either. It's a real challenge. And it takes a huge amount of self-discipline for me not to give them something they want, when I know we can afford it. I love seeing their little faces light up. But I'm able to hold that impulse in check by reminding myself that spoiled, overindulged children often grow up to become troubled, unhappy adults. If I really discipline myself, I am able to keep in mind that the goal is for my children to someday lead happy lives. Then it's a lot easier for me to discipline them and say, "Yes, Mommy loves you, but the answer is still no."

It's extremely important to me that my children don't grow up to be ungrateful. I want to teach them about the value of intangible things—relationships, dreams, experiences, love—and I know that I have to do it when they're still very young. It's critical that they understand just how blessed they are to be born into a family situation where they won't have to worry about so many things. I want them to appreciate what they have and to realize how much they have to be thankful for.

Whenever I'm tempted to complain about how difficult it is to stay focused and disciplined in my life, I think of the story of Helen

Keller. Helen, who became blind and deaf as a result of scarlet fever at a very young age, had grown up a very undisciplined child. Her parents, largely because they didn't know how to deal with her handicap, had spoiled her. When teacher Annie Sullivan, the "Miracle Worker," finally came into her life, Helen was an unruly child; she constantly flew into wild rages and lashed out at those around her. But Annie, a woman of iron will who, but for surgeries, would have been totally blind herself, believed that with patience and discipline, Helen could be turned into something more than the screaming wild child she was.

Annie persevered through all of Helen's tantrums, never losing sight of the goal that she was trying to provide Helen with the tools she needed to someday lead a full and happy life without help from anyone. Year after year, she worked to teach Helen sign language and Braille that would enable her to communicate. In the end, her efforts succeeded in giving Helen both the gift of discipline and the gift of language. It is a truly inspiring story not only about the power of discipline to dramatically improve a child's life, but about what a person can achieve when, despite tremendous obstacles, they learn to cultivate discipline within themselves.

As you move forward on your journey toward happiness, make discipline a cornerstone of your life. It is a trait that you will cherish always, not only for what it allows you to achieve on your personal path to success and satisfaction, but for in the lessons and values it instills in those you love.

THE SIXTH GATEWAY

Health

Since ancient times, the great scholars and sages of every era have observed an essential connection between our health and our happiness. Acclaimed alternative health author Donald Law says, "In the Orient people believed that the basis of all disease was unhappiness. Thus to make a patient happy was to restore him to health." Similarly, the seventeenth-century British philosopher John Locke wrote that, "A sound mind in a sound body, is a short but full description of a happy state in this world." And one of our nation's greatest statesmen, Thomas Jefferson, defined happiness as "not being pained in body nor troubled in mind."

As an athlete, I have always been extremely aware of the correlation between a healthy body and overall emotional well-being. After all, the body houses the mind, and it stands to reason that in order for our minds to function at their best, we need to maintain our physical health. If you've ever sunk to the depths of despair after eating a decadent hot fudge sundae that made you feel five pounds heavier, or felt depressed because you just couldn't shake your winter cold, you know what I mean. It's very hard to focus on the positives in our lives when the very vehicle for our emotions is feeling lousy!

But health doesn't refer only to toned muscles and normal blood pressure, although these things are certainly part of what makes a healthy human being. We're not just flesh and blood—we're mind and spirit, and we need to tend to our minds and souls with the same diligence we apply to firming our abs and biceps. In this chapter, we'll explore what I consider to be the three major components of health: physical, mental and emotional, and spiritual. Only by concentrating equally on each of these areas can we achieve a unified body, mind, and spirit that are each functioning at their best. Trust me: A healthy body is a happy body.

I'm not saying that you can't be happy unless you have perfect health. In fact, very few of us do. Perfection is something that's usually measured by someone attaching a number to it. And while it might be possible to score a perfect 10 in an athletic competition, there's no way to apply that type of measurement to your health. If there were, we'd all be in trouble. There are days, particularly when my allergies are acting up, when I'm definitely a 2. Furthermore, there are thousands of people all over the world who are coping with life-threatening illnesses every day but manage to stay upbeat just the same. Good health, like so many other aspects of happiness, is often a state of mind.

Health is something that you can never win—it's not a competition, and frequently, it is simply beyond our control. One of the first principles of maintaining your good health is to understand and accept this fact. Ironically, it's the opposite of everything I learned in my gymnastics career. Instead of focusing on a specific objective—your ideal weight, the body measurements you most desire—you need to view the game of health in terms of *how* you play it. As I said before, you'll never be able to "win" at health permanently. None of us can. However, there are plenty of things we do to make our journey through life that much easier and more enjoyable by strengthening our bodies and quieting our minds. Being healthy allows you to engage in life to the fullest: swim a few laps in the ocean; play touch football with your kids; *enjoy* that ice cream sundae because you're not worrying about your weight. By adopting a proactive approach to your health, you may well find yourself heading in a straight line toward an equally important goal: your own happiness.

Taking Care of Your Body: Exercise and Nutrition

Keeping your body in prime physical shape is the first step toward good health, and an absolutely essential way of getting in touch with your body and its needs. These days, too many of us are constantly on the go with ever-more-demanding careers that detract from our time with our families and time for ourselves. We're trying to land the corner office at work while being loving parents and attentive friends, and juggling six other activities besides. Given the frantic pace of life today, it's not a surprise that routine exercise and mindful eating usually slip off the day's

I am persuaded that the greater part of our complaints arise from want of exercise.

MARIE DE
RABITIN-CHANTAL

agenda. But I'd like to turn that around and say that given the frantic pace of life today, exercising and eating right are two of the most important things you can do to enhance your well-being and keep up with the rush of life's oncoming challenges. If we neglect our body's physical health through lack of exercise and poor eating habits, it spills over into every aspect of our lives.

I was eighteen when I retired from competitive gymnastics. It was the first time in my life that I was ever truly on my own. I'd been in training for over ten years, and suddenly I was answering only to myself without coaches or parents to guide me. So what did I do? You guessed it: I went crazy with food—cookies, candy, ice cream, you name it. If it wasn't healthy, I ate it. I no longer had any coaches or trainers telling me what I could or couldn't eat. After depriving myself for so many years, I thought I'd earned the right to eat whatever and as much as I wanted.

One thing that I conveniently forgot to take into account was the fact that I'd stopped exercising altogether. I had been an athlete-in-training for so long that I was completely ignorant of what might happen to my body once I stopped being so physically active. So when my food intake increased dramatically, all the weight just stayed on me. With the extra pounds, my energy plummeted. I stopped being able to fit into my favorite clothes, and I felt terribly insecure about my appearance. Here I was, a freshman at the University of Texas, looking to make friends and meet boys, and I didn't even want to go out to parties because I felt so unhappy about my body. Because I never weighed myself, to this day, I still don't know exactly how much I gained. All I can tell you is that I wince whenever I see a photo taken of me during that time.

Of course, the whole time I kept asking myself, why was this happening to *me?* I'd been an athlete all my life, didn't I deserve a break?

In fact, I understood all too well what was going on. When I was actively competing my trainers had explained all the scientific reasons for how we put on or take off weight, but like most teenagers do at some point, I was now stubbornly choosing to ignore what I knew.

The truth is that no one, not even an Olympic athlete, is exempt from gaining weight. It can happen (and eventually does happen) to everybody. If you're a woman, you may have "plumped up" after you had a baby, as I did when Shayla was born. You men know what I'm talking about too, if you've ever had an injury of some kind, say from playing sports or roughhousing with your kids, and you were forced to stop exercising abruptly. Remember what happened? In a very short time you began to notice parts of your body expanding as if you were a bicycle tire and someone was pumping you full of air.

Weight gain, and loss, is like a math problem. If you know the formula—and you're willing to apply it—you can solve it every time. Here's how it works: Your body's weight is determined by the number of calories you eat and then burn off each day. Everything you eat contains calories, and everything you do uses them up, even breathing or sleeping. But if you consume more calories than you burn, they get stored in your body as fat—it's that simple. By adding extra physical activity to your routine, you can use up those excess calories and work off the extra pounds. So:

More Calories + Less Activity = Weight Gain
Same Calories + Same Activity = No Change
Less Calories + More Activity = Weight Loss

It's simple math. And the key to keeping your body slim or losing unwanted weight is equally simple: exercise.

Exercise does a lot more to keep you healthy than just helping you to lose weight. It strengthens your heart muscle, lowers your blood pressure, elevates the level of your so-called good cholesterol while lowering your bad cholesterol at the same time, improves your blood flow, and increases your muscle strength and flexibility. Regular exercise greatly reduces the likelihood of any number of health problems—stroke, heart disease, and osteoporosis, just to name a few. According to a recent study in the *New England Journal of Medicine*, with the proper exercise, women can cut their risk of heart disease by more than *one third*.

It wasn't until well into my freshman year that I finally did something about my weight situation. I was tired of feeling heavy and lethargic, and tired of people looking at me and whispering behind my back. Too often, the whispering was loud enough for me to hear. "Isn't that Mary Lou Retton? Nah, that can't be her, she's not *that* fat." Many people seem to think that because you're a celebrity your life is public domain and they can talk about you freely as if you weren't able to hear them. But even if you're a celebrity, it still hurts.

Finally, it got so bad that I decided that I was ready to get back in shape. I'd done it before; I knew I could do it again. But there was a difference now. This time I would be doing it for myself. Not because it was important to look good in a leotard or to feel lighter in the air while I was performing, or because I had an entire team of talented gymnasts depending on me. This was strictly for *me*. It was a very empowering decision.

There was another major difference. There was no coach to motivate me now, no trainer instructing me. Now I had to do both of those jobs for myself. My first act as my own coach was to enroll myself in a health club, and then to sign myself up for an aerobics class. And, of course, I strongly advised myself to change my eating habits, which we'll discuss in more detail later. I mapped out a program for myself and stuck to it by applying three of the earlier gateways: discipline, a positive attitude, and of course, faith. Within a few months, I felt the change. I could *see* it too. I looked like Mary Lou again.

Here's what I learned from that experience that has shaped the way I approach my health today: If you're motivated enough, it's possible to change your lifestyle and take control of your health without anyone's help. Of course it's great when you *do* have help—a physician or personal trainer, even a good friend—but you really only need *one* person to make it happen: *you.*

I do want to make you an offer, however. Any of you who grew up watching Sylvester the cat and Tweetie bird on Saturday morning cartoons will remember how Sylvester would regularly struggle with whether or not to eat Tweetie bird by having arguments with tiny versions of himself. One was a miniature angel, the other a little devil, and each was perched on a different shoulder of the poor conflicted cat. The devil would whisper and plead and cajole, trying to appeal to Sylvester's worst instincts. The angel was always more gentle in his efforts to exert influence, but he was no less persistent than the devil.

So here's my offer: Whenever you're having trouble staying motivated in your exercise program or you're tempted to grab that candy bar right out of the hand of a little kid because you want it so badly, just picture me as being right there, sitting on your shoulder (I'm a tiny person, so it shouldn't be too hard for you to imagine . . . I'll be the one with the wings). What you can count on me to say to you, every time, is the same thing I said to myself over and over again when I became my own coach: *"You can do it!"*

In 1989, only a few years after I got back into good condition, President George Bush appointed me to serve on the President's Council on Physical Fitness and Sports. It was a terrific honor for me, something I'd wanted to do for a long time. Because physical fitness had provided me with so many opportunities and benefits throughout my life, I'd always looked for ways to share those benefits with others. Because of my history, people pay attention when I talk about fitness training. That gave me a unique opportunity—and, as I saw it, a responsibility—to help other people. If I was able to do only one thing on the President's council, I wanted to make people feel less *afraid* of exercise.

When Arnold Schwarzenegger agreed to come on board and serve as chairman of the President's council, he really raised the profile of the council and our mission. His presence alone gave us instant credibility. I adore Arnold. Now don't laugh, but I think we're a lot alike. We come from similar backgrounds, middle-class families where our parents taught us that we could achieve anything if we believed in ourselves. We're both extremely hard workers—neither of us has ever been given anything in life that we didn't have to earn. And the truth is, neither of us would have wanted it any other way.

Arnold was only thirteen years old and still living in the Austrian town of Graz, where he was born, when he announced to his mother and father, "I want to be the best-built man in the world!" His parents, Gustav and Aurelia Schwarzenegger, reacted just as Lois and Ronnie Retton had in Fairmont, West Virginia, when their daughter announced that she wanted to be like Nadia Comaneci: They shook their heads and smiled.

But Arnold never doubted himself. At fourteen he began an intensive weight training program under the supervision of a former Mr. Austria. The following year he studied psychology in order to learn everything he could about the mind's ability to influence the body. He started competing when he was seventeen and within a year he'd won the most important bodybuilding competition for his age group, Mr. Europe Junior.

When he was twenty-one, Arnold came to America determined to fulfill his dream. He's six two (the same height as Shannon), and when he got to this country he weighed 250 pounds. For months, he spent eight hours a day in a gym, pumping iron and sculpting his body down to the tiniest detail. By the time he was finished, he had a fifty-seven-inch chest, twenty-two-inch biceps, and twenty-eight-inch thighs, and he went on to win an unprecedented seven titles as Mr. Olympia and five more as Mr. Universe. Still only twenty-three, Arnold Schwarzenegger was now officially the "best-built man in the world."

I personally think of Arnold as the Austrian version of Bela. He's an incredible motivator who always tried to "pump us up" to go out there and spread the word about the importance of exercise. Not once during the four years that we served together on the President's Council did we sit around a conference room table just talking about health and fitness. Arnold had no patience for that. Neither did I. We were a new generation of people who actually got out there and worked. His goal as chairman was to visit every state in the country to promote the benefits of physical fitness. It took him all four years, but he did it. On his own time and his own dime.

He also believed that we needed to be aggressively marketing the idea of good health through physical fitness. He conceived an advertising campaign, even writing the slogans himself: "It's Hip to Be Fit" and "Read My Hips: No More Fat." The kick-off of the campaign would be something he called the Great American Work-Out, a huge exercise event to be held on the south lawn of the White House as a way of bringing national media attention to the cause of fitness. Arnold recruited some of the most respected names in sports to participate, including Arthur Ashe, Sam Snead, Bruce Jenner, Scott Hamilton, Dorothy Hamill, Jackie Joyner-Kersee and Carl Lewis. It was an incredible event. Arnold told the crowd that "Fitness is fun, and fitness is for everyone." Then, poking fun at that Hans and Franz parody of him on *Saturday Night Live,* he said, "We vant you all to pump up, to lose those extra inches, to get fit, and to begin right now!"

Then President and Mrs. Bush came out in their warm-up clothes and I led everybody in aerobics. After that, there were individual work-out activities for everybody to do. The President pedaled an exercise bike while hundreds of cameras whirred and clicked. Arnold stood nearby, beaming. He told the reporters that President Bush was "one hundred percent behind physical fitness and in tremendous shape himself." He even added, "I worked out with him once in the White House, and he really made me sweat." President Bush said, "I have been very impressed with the seriousness of our council on fitness and of its chairman, Arnold Schwarzenegger. He's spreading the word that . . . fitness really can enrich the human mind and body."

One of our principal goals on the President's council was trying to restore physical education programs in the schools. So often during budget crunches, they're the first things to get cut. Believe it or not, many of America's youngsters between the ages of five and eight already show at least one of the risk factors for heart disease, such as obesity, elevated cholesterol, or high blood pressure. This is America's secret tragedy. Most students today, male or female, can't run a mile in less than ten minutes or do a single push-up. Physical education classes not only get young people fit by reducing their cholesterol, their stress, and their health risks but at the same time they also increase their stamina, their energy, and their coordination. In addition, they also learn valuable tools for life—discipline, camaraderie, and competition and they gain self-esteem and do better academically. But most important, young people learn how to stay healthy—and because they feel good about themselves, they are less likely to get involved with drugs or alcohol. And the same goes for you.

If you think you don't have the time for exercising, think again. We talked about effective time management in the previous gateway, Discipline, and I urge you to apply your time management skills here. Take a closer look at what you did *yesterday*. Did you watch at least *one* half-hour television show? *Friends? Judge Judy?* If you can find time to do that, then you can spare thirty minutes today to exercise. Take a walk after dinner, spend a half hour playing catch, ride your bike, kick a soccer ball around. There are a hundred different, enjoyable ways to incorporate exercise into your daily life.

Don't think I'm not aware of how hard it is to get started. Remember, I went through it after the Olympics. It's never easy to put that first toe in the water. But you can do it. No matter your age or current health status, it's never too late to start and there are always benefits to be gained. And remember, whenever it gets tough, I'll be right there on your shoulder. Here are some of my tried and true tips:

- Exercise in the *morning*. It will be done and over with and you will start your day feeling energized and guilt-free. Also as the day wears on, your energy wanes and you'll find all kinds of excuses not to exercise. "It's too late to go to the gym," or, "I've had a long day, it won't do me much good when I'm this tired." Trust me, as a mom with two kids, I know—something *always* comes up.

- If you've been inactive for a while, you'll want to go slowly at first, beginning with less strenuous activities such as walking or swimming at an easy pace. Start out doing a half hour of activity two days a week and slowly increase that to an hour four to five days a week over time. You'll build up your stamina gradually that way, without overdoing it.

- When you design your workout, try to do at least thirty minutes of some kind of aerobic activity: walking (briskly, no strolling), bike riding, using the treadmill or the StairMaster. If you don't have access to any machines, don't worry. Here's another quote from Chairman Schwarzenegger that's worth remembering: "[Fitness] doesn't take a lot of money and fancy equipment . . . what it takes is will and opportunity. I've never paid for a push-up or a sit-up in my life and I've done millions."

- Notice the little things you can do during your day while you're out and about: Climb the stairs instead of taking an elevator, or park your car at the *end* of the parking lot (this will also reduce your stress because you won't be fighting for the closest spot anymore). Remember, any exercise, no matter how little, is always better than none.

Tell me what you eat,

and I will tell you

what you are.

JEAN ANTHELME
BRILLAT-SAVARIN

- Find a fellow exerciser to keep you company, and share your successes as you go.

As I said earlier, exercise is only one part of taking care of our bodies. The second half of the equation involves what we put into our bodies as sources of energy and nourishment. You may eat three well-portioned meals a day and avoid snacking, but if you're not eating the right types of foods, you're still doing your body and your health a huge disservice.

As a child, I ate anything—pizza, cookies, ice

cream, you name it. We're an Italian family and my mom is a great cook. She used to pile on huge portions of everything, pasta, meat, sauce—the food was literally hanging off the side of the plate. The only problem was (and still is) that at four nine, I'm the runt of our family. We're all on the small-somewhat-round side, but if I wasn't careful, I would have been the smallest *and* the roundest. It's in my genes. I've had to watch my weight my whole life. And except for that relatively short period of time after the Olympics, I always have. My weight has always hovered around 100 and 105 pounds. I *think*. As I said before, I haven't weighed myself in a very long time. The last time, maybe, was in 1984 at the Olympic training camp in Los Angeles. I was weighed-in at the start of practice and weighed-in at the end. After a six-hour workout, I had lost about two or three pounds . . . just from sweating!

I remember the coaches being so happy. But a few minutes later, I would drink some water to replenish my thirsty body and I gained gain back those two or three pounds. To this day I don't understand the theory behind weigh-ins. I never lost weight. I only lost water.

For two years Bela would say things to me like, "Mary *Lou* (which, in Bela-speak, comes out *Meddy Loo*), is no *good* what you eat. Makes you fat. You should eat only *air*, Mary Lou." He wanted me to be thin enough to really soar when I vaulted over the horse or did back handsprings during my floor routine. Finally, while I was still living in Houston with the Spillers, I completely changed the way I ate. I began to eat chicken and fish all the time, and I had lots of salads, as well as fruits and vegetables. Even at fourteen I didn't think of what I was doing as "going on a diet." I saw it as changing my point of view about food and eating.

Then the strangest thing happened: I discovered that I actually *liked* this new way of eating. Don't get me wrong, I'll always love my mother's cooking: spaghetti and meatballs, pot roast and potatoes, garlic bread dripping with melted cheese. But if I had to now, I could eat only chicken for the rest of my life and be just fine. In fact, two of the recipes I've included in this book are Mary Lou's Crockpot Chicken and Mary Lou's Mexican Chicken.

The difference nutrition can make in your life is truly amazing. Ask Joan Lunden, for one. She's written and spoken about how different her life became after she changed her relationship with food. Joan was forty pounds overweight and approaching her fortieth birthday when she decided to make a change in her lifestyle. What inspired her to do it? Her wake-up call came during an interview she did with a doctor for *Good Morning America.* He gave her a health risk assessment test—on the air—and the results showed her to be at risk for several diseases, including diabetes. But it wasn't just a fear of illness that caused Joan to think seriously about changing her eating habits. There was something bigger that she wanted, something that provided her with an even greater incentive.

"I knew I would have to get healthy if I truly wanted to be happy," she writes in her wonderful book *Joan Lunden's Healthy Living.* "I realized I had to break the cycle of fad diets and weight fluctuation. I wanted to be in control of my energy level, rather than have my energy level control my daily life. I lost almost fifty pounds, I lowered my health risk, I put physical activity and fun back into my life. I turned my life around."

"Fad diets." Low carbohydrates. No carbohydrates. Carbohydrate addicts. Do any of these methods really work? According to Dr. Mary Michael Levitt, the answer is a big . . . *fat* . . . *"no."* She asserts, ". . . 96% of those who lose weight on these diets gain it back . . . Dieting ignores the development of healthy eating solutions. Instead, strict eating rules (the core of most diet programs) impede the necessary recovery process for disease and addiction."

I'll never go on a "diet" because to me, a diet implies deprivation. I don't believe that it's ever healthy to eliminate a food group or starve yourself just to lose weight. There's so much more to food than calories. I believe in eating nutritious meals without letting myself or my family feel guilty or deprived. I don't even own a scale because I don't want my or my children's definition of health to be linked with a certain weight or dress size. As Dr. Levitt says, "For lasting weight loss to occur a person needs to change his lifestyle attitudes and response to food."

As I said earlier, I had to do that for a second time in my life when I was a freshman at the University of Texas and I'd launched my brief one-woman rebellion against nutrition. I thought that all I'd have to do was wave my white flag at those evil pizzas (they just kept *showing up* at my door) and bang! I'd immediately be eating healthy meals again. I quickly discovered that it wasn't going to be quite that easy. You'd think that once a person had already developed sensible eating habits — especially at a young age — he or she would have no trouble picking them right back up again. Like riding a bicycle, right? I can tell you from personal experience that while it may be true for some people, it wasn't true for me.

At that point I met with a nutritionist who, as it turned out, taught me a lot of things I thought I knew (but didn't really) about maintaining a healthy lifestyle. One of the first things I realized was that I'd been dreading going back to the days of eating "Bela Air" for breakfast. I didn't want to deprive myself anymore, but the nutritionist made me understand, really for the first time in my life, that it wasn't how much I ate, it was *what* I ate that was important. He put me on a program of eating five small healthy meals a day. You speed up your metabolism by eating five smaller meals, as opposed to the three large ones. It's back to that basic math formula again: Every time you eat something, your body goes to work to use up the calories. So it follows that the more *often* you eat (ideally small portions of only healthy food), the more your metabolism kicks in and the more calories you're burning off.

The other thing I came to understand was the role that genetics plays in determining the size and shape of your body. Unfortunately, many of us have totally unrealistic and unhealthy expectations about how we will look after dieting and exercising, and inevitably, we're disappointed. I always knew that I wasn't born with a "skinny" gene, so trying to look like Kate Moss was never an option for me. And I was fine with that! My goal was pretty simple, but therefore achievable. I told the nutritionist that I wasn't interested in a "number." I just wanted to get back down to a weight that seemed comfortable to me. A natural weight, a healthy weight, a weight at which I would be feeling good. As Dr. Levitt says, "The most effective weight loss approach is one that the client can apply daily, and that specifically addresses what needs to be done in each individual situation. This approach places responsibility for changing behavior and losing weight on the *person*, not the program."

My sessions with the nutritionist, combined with my pre-Olympic experience, convinced me that I'd never again use deprivation as a means to lose weight. And over the last twelve years, my entire approach to eating and food has remained consistent with two basic ideas.

1. Eat five small portions of healthy food every day.
2. Don't try to be who you're not.

I've used this program for a good long while now, and it's amazing how well it works. I'm able to maintain my weight and keep my cholesterol down, all without ever feeling deprived. Shannon and the girls follow it as well, and I haven't heard any complaints. I encourage you to give it a try. (Of course, that second idea will work for you in a lot of other areas of your life, besides just eating.)

Here's how I handle my meals during a typical week:

- Monday through Friday: During the week, I really focus on eating well-balanced healthy meals. I stick with low-fat, low-calorie foods such as chicken (without the skin, of course), fish, vegetables, fruit, pasta, and bread. Not the whole loaf, of course—portion sizes count. And, yes, you will have to pass on using any butter or olive oil with it. Try to steer clear of unhealthy condiments and extras.

- How you prepare food is very important. When you're sautéing, use a vegetable spray, chicken broth, or fruit juice. They're all great substitutes for oil or butter, which we only use to prevent what we're cooking from sticking to the skillet. That's one extra source of calories we can do without! The added benefit of healthy meals is that, in general, cooking and cleanup are much easier. Steaming and sautéing take far less time and energy than deep-frying, stewing, and other old-fashioned forms of cooking. And don't ever eat more than you need. When you feel full, stop—it's as simple as that. As the saying goes, we should "eat to live, not live to eat."

- Drink water: Water is the best friend your healthy body has. It flushes toxins out of your system which, among countless other benefits, will improve your energy level and your complexion. You should try to drink between six and eight 8-ounce glasses a day. Six to eight glasses may sound like a lot, but there are numerous easy ways to increase your water intake. When you're hungry between meals, pour yourself a glass of water. You'll feel full and be able to avoid snacking. If you're on your way to work out, have a glass of water *before* exercising. You'll find that it keeps you operating at peak performance. Water is one of the easiest ways to nourish our bodies and improve our overall health—and best of all, it's free.

- Drink tea: I've always been an avid tea drinker and last year I agreed to serve as a spokeswoman for Lipton. Before I did, I sat down with the Lipton people and they really gave me an education on the health benefits that you can get out of just one little cup of tea. Fresh-brewed, unsweetened tea is 100 percent natural and contains no fat, sugar, or calories. But did you also know that tea (both black and green), like many fruits and vegetables, is a natural source of flavonoids? A flavonoid is a plant product that's found in onions as well as tea leaves. Flavonoids act as antioxidants in the body, neutralizing harmful chemicals that damage cells and can lead to illnesses such as heart attacks, strokes, and cancer. In fact, research done at the Harvard Medical School shows that people who have a cup or more of tea a day reduce their risk of a heart attack by 44 percent, as compared to non-tea drinkers.

    If you're a tea drinker already, congratulations! You've been doing something healthy all these years. For you coffee drinkers, I've got one question. Isn't it teatime?

- Take vitamins and supplements: Do I believe in vitamins? You bet I do. I take them every day. Even people with healthy eating habits can catch a cold now and then. Whenever I feel a cold coming on, I increase my level of vitamin C immediately. Work with a doctor or nutritionist to find out which vitamins or supplements best suit your needs, and how often you should take them.

- Saturday or Sunday: I eat whatever I want on one of these days. After all, *it's the weekend!* And you should splurge. You've eaten well the entire week and are probably sick of eating chicken breasts and broccoli. Or maybe you're craving something sweeter than an apple. Whatever it is, *have it.* Set aside one day a week to not deprive yourself of the foods you want. Come Monday morning, you'll be motivated and charged up to restart your healthy eating program. Knowing that one day out of every week I can eat whatever I want enables me to be sensible all through the week. The whatever-I-want is a reward. For me—it's usually pizza (with everything on it except mushrooms), french fries, or chips and salsa. (I don't have much of a sweet tooth, so a big ol' chocolate cookie will usually do it for me when it comes to dessert.) Best of all, knowing that you've given yourself the freedom to eat whatever you want on that one day won't leave you feeling guilty after you indulge. Furthermore, by allowing yourself to eat those "forbidden" foods, your desire for them diminishes. You won't have to torture yourself with statements like, "Oh, man, I wish I could have that piece of chocolate cake." Instead, *have it.* When you give yourself the freedom to choose, you take away any guilt. And, at the same time, you'll strengthen your long-term resolve to keep eating smart.

Mary Lou's Weekly Plan for Healthy Eating

MONDAY THROUGH FRIDAY

Breakfast 3 or 4 scrambled egg whites or Egg Beaters
(use Pam spray)
1 slice whole wheat toast/no butter
Tea

Snack Fat-free yogurt with 2 tablespoons raw oats
and raisins mixed in

Lunch 3- to 4-ounce piece of lean chicken or fish
1 cup steamed vegetables
1 cup rice or pasta or 1 medium potato/
no butter

Snack A piece of fruit or fruit smoothie

Dinner Same as lunch (alternating between chicken
and fish)

SATURDAY OR SUNDAY

Pick one of these days to splurge:
Eat whatever you want!
On the other day, stick to the above regimen.

Rather than focusing on what you shouldn't eat (which is never any fun), it's much more interesting and enjoyable to focus on what you *should eat*. I've included eighteen of my favorite healthy recipes—you'll find that many have a touch of real Tex-Mex flavor—to help you get started on your new eating program. I think you'll find that they're all truly delicious and enjoyable. Trust me—you'll hardly know you're eating healthfully.

Pasta Primavera with Shrimp

Serves 2

1 cup low-fat cottage cheese
10 medium shrimp, peeled and deveined
1 small zucchini, thinly sliced (about 1 cup)
1 medium red pepper, thinly sliced (about 3/4 cup)
1 small carrot, shredded (about 1/2 cup)
½ cup finely chopped green onions
¼ teaspoon salt
½ teaspoon ground red pepper
2 cups cooked fusilli pasta
One 4-ounce can peas, drained
½ cup evaporated skim milk

1. Place the cottage cheese in a blender and process until smooth. Reserve ⅓ cup and refrigerate the rest for another use.

2. Spray a medium skillet with nonstick vegetable cooking spray and place over high heat. Add the shrimp, zucchini, carrot, red pepper, green onions, salt, and red pepper. Cook, stirring, for 8 minutes, or until the shrimp turn pink.

3. Stir in the pasta and drained peas. Cook, stirring, for 3 minutes. Remove from the heat, transfer to a glass bowl, and set aside.

4. To same skillet, over high heat, add the milk and the reserved blended cottage cheese and bring to a boil. Cook, stirring, for 5 minutes, or until the sauce thickens.

5. Add the shrimp and pasta mixture and cook for 1 minute more.

Note: For variety, substitute turkey or chicken breasts for the shrimp.

Sautéed Chicken with Mushrooms and Peapods

Serves 2

1 teaspoon granulated garlic

½ teaspoon paprika

¼ teaspoon salt

¼ teaspoon ground white pepper

¼ teaspoon ground thyme

2 boneless, skinless single chicken breasts, skinned
   and cut into 1-inch strips

1 tablespoon cornstarch

1½ cups chicken stock or water

1 cup thinly sliced fresh mushrooms

1 cup fresh peapods

½ cup finely chopped green onions

1 tablespoon dehydrated onion

½ teaspoon browning and seasoning sauce

1. In a small bowl, combine the garlic, paprika, salt, white pepper, and thyme. Mix well and sprinkle over the chicken.

2. Spray a large skillet with nonstick vegetable spray and place over high heat. Add the chicken and sauté for 10 minutes, stirring often and scraping the bottom of the skillet with a wooden spoon.

3. Dissolve the cornstarch in 1 cup of the stock and add it to the mixture. Stir in the mushrooms, peapods, green onions, dehydrated onion, browning sauce, and the remaining ½ cup stock. Reduce the heat to low, cover, and simmer for 30 minutes, stirring often.

Hot and Sour Red Snapper

Serves 4

1 teaspoon granulated garlic

¼ teaspoon salt

¼ teaspoon ground white pepper

¼ teaspoon ground red pepper

¼ teaspoon ground oregano

¼ teaspoon ground thyme

1 pound red snapper fillet, or any firm white-fleshed fish

½ cup unsweetened orange juice

½ cup barbecue sauce

4 tablespoons lemon juice

1 tablespoon honey

1 tablespoon green onions

2 tablespoons very finely chopped fresh parsley

1. Preheat the oven to 350°F.

2. In a small bowl, mix together the garlic, salt, white and red peppers, oregano, and thyme. Sprinkle the seasoning mixture on both sides of the fish.

3. Spray an 8-inch square baking dish with nonstick vegetable spray. Arrange the fish fillets in the dish and set aside.

4. In a small saucepan over high heat, bring to a boil the remaining ingredients except for the green onions and parsley. Boil for 10 minutes, stirring often.

5. Remove the sauce from the heat and spoon over the fish, then top with the green onions and parsley. Bake, uncovered, for 20 minutes or until the fish flakes easily with a fork.

Cajun Chicken Breasts

Serves 4

4 boneless, skinless single chicken breasts
½ tablespoon olive oil
2 tablespoons lemon juice
½ teaspoon chili powder
½ teaspoon paprika
½ teaspoon cayenne
½ teaspoon dried basil
2 cloves garlic, crushed
Salt and freshly ground pepper to taste

1. Rinse the chicken and pat dry. Trim off any excess fat.

2. In a mixing bowl, combine the oil, lemon juice, seasonings, and garlic. Add the chicken and marinate for 12 hours, covered, in the refrigerator.

3. Preheat the oven to 300°F. Remove the chicken from the marinade and arrange in a single layer on a foil-lined 10 × 15 × 1-inch rimmed baking sheet. Pour marinade over and around chicken.

4. Bake, uncovered, for 20 minutes, turning the chicken pieces over at half time. Baste occasionally with the pan juices. When done, the chicken will be springy when lightly touched. If overcooked, the chicken will be tough. Serve without pan juices.

Chunky Ratatouille

Serves 6 to 8

2 onions, thinly sliced
1 tablespoon olive oil
3 cloves garlic, crushed
1 small eggplant (about ¾ pound), cut into 1" chunks
1 green pepper, cut into thin strips
2 red peppers, cut into thin strips
2 medium zucchini, sliced
2 large ripe tomatoes, cut into chunks
One 8-ounce can tomato sauce
1 tablespoon balsamic vinegar
Pinch of chile flakes
½ teaspoon chili powder
⅓ teaspoon ground oregano
½ teaspoon mixed Italian seasoning
1 teaspoon sugar
2 tablespoons fresh basil, chopped, or 1 teaspoon dried

1. Sauté the onions in the oil on medium heat for 3 or 4 minutes. Add the garlic and sauté briefly. Add the eggplant. Sauté for 5 minutes longer, stirring occasionally. Add the peppers and zucchini and sauté for 5 minutes.

2. Add the remaining ingredients. Bring to a boil, reduce the heat, and simmer, covered, for 25 minutes longer, until the vegetables are tender. Stir occasionally.

Mary Lou's Crockpot Chicken

Serves 4 to 6
1 whole chicken, (8 to 10 pounds)
Salt and pepper to taste
One 14.5-ounce can chicken broth
2 bay leaves
3 cloves garlic

1. In the morning, clean the chicken and rub the salt and pepper into the outside skin.

2. Place the chicken in the crockpot. Add the chicken broth, bay leaves, and garlic.

3. Set the crockpot on low and cook for 6 to 8 hours. When you return home in the evening, your meal is ready and waiting! Remove and discard the bay leaves before serving with roasted potatoes or rice.

Glazed Apricot Mustard Chicken Breasts

Serves 6

6 single skinless chicken breasts (with bone)
¼ cup Dijon mustard
¼ cup apricot jam
1 tablespoon honey
1 teaspoon olive oil
Freshly ground pepper and paprika to taste
One 14-ounce can (398 ml) water-packed apricots,
    drained, to garnish

1. Line a 10 × 15-inch baking sheet with foil and spray with non-stick vegetable spray. Remove the skin from the chicken. Trim off any excess fat.

2. In a small bowl, combine the mustard, jam, honey, oil, and rosemary. Mix well. Rub the chicken with the mustard glaze, reserving any leftover glaze.

3. Arrange the chicken bone side down on the baking sheet. Sprinkle lightly with pepper and paprika.

4. Preheat the oven to 350°F. Bake the chicken, uncovered, on the middle rack of the oven for 45 minutes, brushing it with the reserved glaze during the last 15 minutes of cooking. When done, the chicken will be glazed and golden.

5. Arrange the chicken on a serving platter and garnish with drained apricots.

Mary Lou's Quick-'n'-Easy Pot Roast

Serves 4 to 6

2 pounds lean roast beef

One 14.5-ounce can beef stock

One 14.5-ounce can diced tomatoes

1 cup diced celery

1 cup diced carrots

1 cup diced onion

2 bay leaves

5 peppercorns

3 cloves garlic, minced

1 teaspoon salt

1. Spray the bottom of a large Dutch oven or soup pot with vegetable spray.

2. In the Dutch oven, combine all the ingredients. Bring to a boil over high heat, then reduce the heat to medium-high. Cook uncovered for 3 hours.

Mary Lou's Mexican Chicken

Serves 4

One 15-ounce can black beans
One 15-ounce can pinto beans
4 boneless, skinless, single chicken breasts
3 tablespoons minced garlic
1 teaspoon chili powder
1 tablespoon garlic salt
1 tablespoon pepper
One 20-ounce jar picante sauce
½ cup shredded Cheddar cheese

1. Preheat the oven to 400°F.

2. Drain both cans of beans, and rinse with water. Mix the beans together and place in the bottom of a 13 × 9 × 2-inch cooking pan.

3. Lay the chicken breasts on top of the beans. Spread the minced garlic over the chicken. Sprinkle the chicken with chili powder, garlic, salt, and pepper. Cover the chicken with the entire jar of picante sauce.

4. Bake the chicken, uncovered, for 30 to 40 minutes. When finished, sprinkle with the cheese and serve.

Quickie Chicken Noodle and Vegetable Soup

Serves 4

4 cups chicken broth (preferably homemade)
2 boneless, skinless chicken breasts, finely diced, or 1 cup diced
    cooked chicken
1 cup linguine, cooked *al dente*
1 cup frozen mixed vegetables
Pepper to taste
1 tablespoon minced fresh dill or 1 teaspoon dried
2 green onions, finely chopped

1. Place the broth in a large saucepan and bring to a boil. Add the chicken, noodles, and vegetables. Simmer 7 or 8 minutes, or until the chicken is cooked.

2. Add the pepper. Garnish with the dill and green onions.

No-Fry French Fries

Serves 6

6 baking potatoes (Idaho or Russet)
1 tablespoon canola or olive oil
1 egg white
Salt and pepper to taste
Basil, cayenne, paprika, and/or garlic powder to taste

1. Preheat the oven to 400°F. Spray a rimmed baking sheet with non-stick vegetable spray. Peel the potatoes (or scrub well). Cut into ¼-inch strips. (If you have time, soak the strips in ice water for 20 to 30 minutes for crispier fries. Drain well and pat dry.)

2. In a medium bowl, beat the oil with the egg white until frothy.

3. Coat the potatoes with the oil/egg white mixture. Spread in a single layer on a baking sheet. Sprinkle with seasonings.

4. Bake in the lower third of the oven for 35 to 45 minutes, or until brown and crispy, stirring once or twice. Serve immediately.

Spicy Corn Salad

Serves 4

1 cup low-fat cottage cheese

One 10-ounce package frozen whole-kernel corn or 8 ears fresh
   corn kernels, cut off the cob (about 2 cups)

½ cup finely chopped onion

½ cup finely chopped green bell pepper

½ cup finely chopped red bell pepper

1 teaspoon finely chopped pimento

1 teaspoon finely chopped fresh parsley

¼ teaspoon salt

⅛ teaspoon ground white pepper

½ teaspoon ground black pepper

1 tablespoon balsamic vinegar

1 tablespoon reduced-calorie mayonnaise

1. Place the cottage cheese in a blender and process until smooth.
Reserve 1 tablespoon of the pureed cottage cheese; refrigerate the remainder for another use.

2. In a medium saucepan, cook the corn according to the directions on the package. Drain and set aside. For fresh corn, cook in 2 cups water until tender, about five minutes.

3. In a separate bowl, combine the corn, reserved pureed cottage cheese, and all the remaining ingredients, stirring to mix well.

4. Cover and refrigerate 6 hours before serving.

No-Guilt Chocolate Cake

Serves 18

2¼ cups flour

2 cups sugar

⅓ cup cocoa

1½ teaspoons baking powder

1½ teaspoons baking soda

¼ teaspoon salt

¼ cup brewed coffee

¾ cup orange juice

2 eggs plus 2 egg whites

¾ cup unsweetened applesauce

¼ cup canola oil

1. Preheat the oven to 350°F. Combine all the dry ingredients in a food processor with plastic blade and process until well blended, about 10 seconds.

2. Add the coffee, orange juice, eggs, egg whites, and applesauce. Start the processor and add the oil through the feed tube while the machine is running. Process the batter for 45 seconds.

3. Pour the batter into a 12-cup Bundt pan sprayed with nonstick vegetable spray. Bake for 55 to 60 minutes, until you can insert a toothpick into the cake and it comes out clean.

4. Cool for 20 minutes before removing the cake from the pan.

Fruit and Yogurt Smoothie

Serves 1

½ cup plain or vanilla yogurt
½ cup sliced fruit of your choice
¼ teaspoon vanilla extract
2 or 3 ice cubes
1 to 2 teaspoons sugar or artificial sweetener

In a blender or food processor fitted with a plastic blade, blend the first four ingredients until smooth. Add the sugar or sweetener to taste.

Apricot Orange Cream Smoothie

Serves 1

4 fresh apricots, halved
1 peeled orange, sectioned
1 frozen banana, chunked
1 tablespoon chopped pecans
1 tablespoon shredded coconut
1 cup apple juice

In a blender or food processor fitted with a steel blade, blend all the ingredients until smooth.

Berry Nectarine Smoothie

Serves 2

2 nectarines, peeled, pitted, and chopped
1 frozen banana
1 pint berries of your choice
1 handful pitted dates
1 teaspoon ground cinnamon
1 cup apple juice

In a blender or food processor fitted with steel blade, blend the ingredients until smooth.

Summer Peach Smoothie

Serves 2

2 cups pitted and chunked fresh peaches
2 frozen bananas, chunked
1 tablespoon shredded coconut
1 cup apple juice

In a blender or food processor fitted with steel blade, blend the ingredients until smooth.

Pineapple Berry Smoothie

Serves 1

½ cup pineapple chunks
½ cup blueberries
½ cup crushed ice

In a blender or food processor, blend the ingredients until smooth.

There's one last thing I want you to keep in mind as you're trying to make any kind of improvements in your life or lifestyle. I use the word "improvements" deliberately, because real change is a lifelong process—it's not governed by the clock or the calendar. That's why it's a good idea to set simple realistic goals for yourself along the way, goals that are actually achievable. Then you'll almost always have something to feel good about.

It's easy to focus on failure, but congratulating yourself for your successes—no matter how small—is a much healthier way to live. If your exercise program is going well, treat yourself to something: a manicure or tickets to a baseball game. If you've accomplished one of your short-term goals in eating more healthfully—say you've managed *not* to give in over Thanksgiving—buy yourself a bouquet of fresh flowers or go to the movies with a friend, even on a weeknight.

But remember, if you're tempted to buy the buttered popcorn, don't do it! I'll be right there on your shoulder . . .

Tending to Mind and Heart

As I mentioned earlier, the good health of your body isn't the only thing you'll need in order to cross through the sixth gateway of happiness. Your mind and your spirit need to be equally healthy too. As anyone who has ever had a broken heart knows, our everyday ailments aren't always physical—and taking care of our emotional health and well-being is essential to leading a balanced and happy life.

A cheerful heart is good medicine, but a crushed spirit dries up the bones.

PROVERBS 17:22

Because we can't measure our state of mind as precisely as we can our waistline, or identify an emotional break anywhere near as easily as we can spot a broken bone, we often fail to treat our mental and emotional health with the same care we give to our physical well-being. A lot of people—you might be one of them—just shrug their shoulders and think it's normal if they're tired all the time, even when they've had enough sleep. Or they think the blues they've been unable to shake for several weeks is something "everybody goes through"—they've just got to "tough it out."

As someone who's "toughed it out" through lots of physical injuries in my life, let me say this to you as clearly as I know how: It's *not* the same thing. Whenever your emotions are in a state of upheaval, for whatever reason—the death of a loved one, a change in job, a move to a new home, or even, as was dramatically the case last year for my friend Marie Osmond, the birth of a new baby—the consequences can be hugely disruptive to your journey toward happiness. That's why it's so important that we develop tools to care for our minds and souls, the same way we care for our muscles by going for a run.

In 1998 I traveled to Nagano, Japan, as part of the United States delegation to the Winter Olympics. Tipper Gore, wife of Vice President Al Gore, was the head of our delegation and we were lucky enough to be able to use his plane, *Air Force Two,* to make the trip. Tipper is a wonderful woman, and we had great fun traveling together. One of the things I admire most about her, however, is the personal commitment she's made to the cause of mental health in America. Since her husband was elected vice president, she's spoken widely about the issue and was candid in revealing her own treatment for depression, which resulted from a near-fatal automobile accident involving the Gores' then six-year-old son. The little boy was holding on to his father's hand, and they were about to cross a street, when he suddenly pulled loose and ran in front of a car. Neither of his parents had time to react; they could only watch in shock and horror as it happened in front of them. Honestly, I don't know what I would do if something like that ever happened to one of our girls. I can't even begin to imagine how I'd cope.

Sometimes it's incredibly difficult for us to tell how other people are feeling, even if it's someone very close to us. Marie Osmond has been my friend for almost ten years. She and John Schneider (Bo from the *Dukes of Hazzard*) are the cofounders of the Children's Miracle Network, the wonderful charity I devote much of my time and energy to supporting year round. Marie has seven children, ranging in age from seventeen to the youngest, Matthew, who's almost a year old now.

I'd always thought Marie had managed to find that perfect balance between family and her career in show business. I once even asked her to share the secret of how she managed to do it all so well. I remember her telling me, "You've got to love what you're doing." She made it sound so easy, and I always looked to her as a role model when trying to find the proper balance between family and career in my own life.

So I was completely stunned when last fall, along with the rest of the world, I saw Marie on television describing to Oprah Winfrey exactly what happened shortly after Matthew was born.

"I basically gave the baby to the baby-sitter, got in my car, and just left, never thinking I would come back, not really knowing where I was going or what I was doing," she told Oprah. "I just really felt that my kids would be better off if they didn't have a mother."

Marie says she drove for over twenty-four hours until her husband finally reached her on her cell phone and tried to persuade her to pull over. Fortunately, she was so exhausted that she eventually agreed to check into a motel. If she hadn't done so, she might never have received help for what was later diagnosed as postpartum depression, a little-discussed emotional illness that affects millions of new mothers every year. Many are either too ill to recognize its symptoms or, when they do, are too ashamed to admit it to anyone.

The truth is, I've had to deal with it too. It was right after my second daughter, McKenna, was born. Not as severely as Marie, thank the Lord, but it was an extremely difficult time for me. The hormones take over and you literally feel like you're losing your mind. Crying all the time, questioning if you can handle the new baby, if you did the right thing having this child. I was terrified, wondering if I'd ever feel like my old self again and feeling as if I were simply going to crumble under the pressure of raising a second daughter. It was truly horrible and at the time I wasn't entirely sure of how to handle the situation. I'm Mary Lou Retton, after all, and I'm *supposed* to have a positive attitude about everything. Everyone knows that about me. And they always expect to see me smile, no matter what.

Then, without warning, I couldn't do it. Not only could I not smile, I couldn't stop crying. It felt as if I'd never again have another happy day in my life. That's the scary part about depression or any psychological illness. When you have it, you think you'll never get through it. Even more frightening is that it's often completely beyond your control. I prayed and prayed to God to give me the strength to pull myself together. I can even remember having actual conversations with myself through the tears: "Mary Lou, these are your *hormones*. You're *not* going crazy and you can handle this. Stop! Snap out of it! Get yourself under control!"

Of course I now understand that postpartum depression doesn't work that way; it can't. I was very fortunate in that I didn't have full-blown postpartum depression. I had what's called postpartum "blues," which affects 70–80 percent of new mothers and typically lasts only a few weeks (postpartum depression is more intense than the "blues" and, left untreated, can last much longer).—In just three weeks my body straightened itself out. One day, like a cloud that had passed in front of the sun, it was suddenly gone. Almost as quickly as it had appeared. And I was myself again.

So many women endure much more difficult experiences. When I watched Marie Osmond's appearance on *Oprah* last fall, my heart just went out to her. I thought to myself, "There but for the grace of God . . ."

Marie showed such bravery in being willing to come forward and talk openly about her personal struggle with postpartum depression. Like Mrs. Gore, her example will undoubtedly provide support and encouragement to countless others who need medical care and might otherwise be too afraid or ashamed to seek it out.

Postpartum depression is just one form of emotional imbalance that can dramatically impact our lives. It may be something as life-altering as a true mental illness or merely a bout of the winter blues that drains our energy and makes us grumpy. Very few of us are immune to the external pressures of daily life. As human beings, we are blessed with the ability to feel and sometimes our feelings get the better of us. If a conflict with a coworker is making us crazy, we may find we're unable to get a good night's sleep. If someone hurts our feelings we may suddenly lose our appetite even if we're sitting over a plate of our favorite food. The important thing is that we learn to acknowledge and treat these emotions, instead of burying them deep inside us and hoping they disappear.

It's crucial that we find ways to cope with everyday emotional stresses so that our minds and hearts remain healthy. One effective way to take your mind off whatever is bringing you down is to take a break from whatever is bothering you and do something to help someone else. Whether it's volunteering your time for a worthy cause, working with the teens group in your church, or just doing a favor for a friend, stepping outside of your immediate world often allows you to see that bigger picture we talked about in Attitude. One of the first things you might discover is that your own problems aren't nearly as important as you thought they were. This happens to me whenever I do volunteer work for the Children's Miracle Network, which funds hospital care for kids around the country.

The time I spend working with CMN improves my emotional health in two immediate ways. Helping those wonderful children is such an amazing gift for all of us who participate. The children are so brave and, quite often, they're wise beyond their years because they've been through so much at such a young age. Visiting them, talking to them, and sharing their hopes and fears create a win-win situation. They love the entertainment and support that CMN provides, and I am reminded to thank the Lord for blessing me and Shannon with two healthy, beautiful children. The rest of life's little problems — the fact that they overcharged me at the dry cleaners or that the girls' squabbling this morning gave me a headache — seem pretty

The happiest people

are those who think

the most interesting

thoughts. Those who

decide to use leisure

as a means of mental

development, who love

good music, good books,

good pictures, good

company, good conversa-

tion, are the happiest

people in the world.

And they are not only

happy in themselves,

they are the cause of

happiness in others.

WILLIAM LYON
PHELPS

insignificant by comparison. Then when you're ready to come back and address them, you're likely to deal with them in a much healthier fashion.

Providing nourishment—"brain food"—for our minds is also a tremendously important part of maintaining our mental health. Anyone who's ever read to a small child at bedtime ("One *more* story, Mommy. Please!") knows what a precious, wonderful thing it is to see the look of pure joy on a small face every time a new word or a new idea is absorbed. Although we're not as aware of it as adults, that kind of mental stimulation remains important throughout our entire lifetime. It contributes enormously to a healthy mind, which, in turn, enables us to better appreciate and enjoy the things in life that give us happiness: our families, our friends, all the people we love.

One idea that I've really come to embrace over the past few years is that education doesn't come to an end when we graduate from high school or college. It's an ongoing process that we should make an effort to incorporate into our lives at every stage. The great thing about education as an adult is that it's no longer restricted to potentially boring lectures or lengthy term papers—you can study whatever you want, on your own time. You can visit a museum and get a taste of art history or read a wonderful captivating book on a topic you've always had an interest in. You might learn a bit more about our country's history by chatting with a relative who served in one of the recent wars. Or, you can be more direct and sign up for a continuing education class. I have friends my age or older who are taking classes in French cooking or studying Spanish in anticipation of taking a trip to Mexico. Exercising your brain feels every bit as good as a grueling workout at the gym—and it makes every aspect of life that much more exciting.

Now it's your turn. What do's and don'ts can you think of that will promote mental and emotional well-being? Take a few moments to reflect on your life: the activities and the people in it. Try to pinpoint the forces that generate stress and emotional discomfort. Then, try to come up with tools you can use to deal with these activities and people in a healthy, reasonable manner. You'll be amazed at how much healthier—and happier—you'll feel once you begin tending to emotional stress and enhancing your peace of mind.

- *Positive words*—One very effective way that we can prevent negative thoughts from taking over is by refraining from saying them out loud. Words are powerful, and when we give voice to our negative emotions we reinforce them and give them power over us. They set our tone, they affect our mood, and they convey our negative sentiments to others. On a rainy day, if you go around muttering about how terrible the weather is, you're likely to have a much more unpleasant day than if you say, "Well, maybe somewhere they *need* the rain."

- *Meditate*—Ten years ago meditation was something practiced only by aging hippies and Asian spiritual leaders. Today, thousands of Americans, from celebrities to athletes, are using this wonderfully simple technique to relieve stress and lower blood pressure. I've found that the Bible provides wonderful material for this practice, and we've already been encouraged to "meditate on [the Word of God] day and night." (Joshua 1:8) Since the goal of meditation is to relax through gentle, regulated breathing and to cleanse our minds of all our worries and anxieties, what better way to do so than by meditating on God's teachings and infinite love? In our fast-paced overly stimulated world of cellular phones and satellite dishes with hundreds of television channels, meditation can be a truly enjoyable way to promote physical and emotional well-being.

- *Get a good night's rest*—Even people in wonderful health can't go for too long without enough sleep. A sleep deficit can weaken your immune system, leaving you more open not only to physical illness but to irritability and mood-swings as well. We all know how easy it is to be grouchy and unpleasant when we're operating on four hours of sleep. Things that may not cause us stress under ordinary circumstances can send us through the roof if we're over-tired. In contrast, a good night's rest is a body- and a mind builder. If you're getting less than your body needs, try making it to bed a half-hour earlier each night until you gradually reach the optimal eight hours. I promise you'll see a difference.

- *Give yourself a break*—Something that most of us don't get enough of is time for ourselves. We're constantly being pulled in many different directions, by our families, by our jobs, and by our friends. Even though it's important to give all of them the time and attention they deserve, it's just as important to take some time for ourselves, time to unwind. Just like when we were kids, we need to take a "time-out" every so often (although this is a reward, not a punishment - maybe it's more like "recess"). I know it's easier said than done, but if you set your mind to it, it's really not as hard as you think. It doesn't have to be anything terribly creative, and it doesn't have to take a lot of time. It may be as simple as taking a walk, going to dinner with friends, seeing a movie, or just relaxing in the sun with a cup of peppermint tea. Of course, curling up in the bathtub with your new book isn't bad, either! It's not so much what you do, just the fact that you do *something* solely for yourself. Allotting yourself this special time allows you to regroup and get your energy back. Surprisingly, these small rituals will allow you more energy and enthusiasm for everything and everyone else around you.

Nourishing Your Soul

Although earlier in this book, in the gateway on Faith, we talked about cultivating a personal relationship with God and the profound impact this type of relationship and spiritual sustenance can have on our overall sense of well-being, it would be impossible for me to write about Health without addressing the importance of both faith and prayer to our physical well-being. Obviously our spiritual life is greatly enhanced by regularly practiced prayer and a continued deep connection with our faith, but more and more doctors and scientists are acknowledging the legitimate value of spirituality in contributing to our physical health as well. I think that many of us recognize how faith and spirituality impact on us in a physical sense. Think about the feeling of safety and serenity that washes over you as you enter a church or chapel. The

I'm fulfilled in what I do . . . I never thought that a lot of money or fine clothes—the finer things of life—would make you happy. My concept of happiness is to be filled in a spiritual sense.

CORETTA
SCOTT KING

213

noisy chaos of the outside world fades away and our bodies relax as we take in the softly colored light from the stained-glass windows and listen to the quiet strains of music or the hushed whispers of other parishioners. Houses of worship are wonderful places of sanctuary where we can distance ourselves from our outside cares and reflect on what's important to us. Dr. Alexis Carrel, one of the pioneers of modern medicine, eloquently asserts, "As a physician, I have seen men, after all other therapy had failed, lifted out of disease and melancholy by the serene effort of prayer." Prayer and worship, like meditation, slow our breathing, lower our blood pressure, and allow us to connect with something greater than ourselves. These acts not only relax our physical bodies, they lift our spirits as well.

A poll taken in 1999 shows that an astonishing 99 percent of physicians in the United States believe that religious belief contributes to the healing of the sick and over 70 percent believe that, if they are requested to do so, they should join their patients in prayers for healing. In his book *The Healing Power of Faith,* Dr. Harold Koenig suggests that there are significant, measurable health benefits to being a person of religious faith and that religious people tend to live longer, healthier lives. "They're a lot less likely to have diastolic hypertension," says Dr. Koenig, "[a] kind of blood pressure disease or hypertension which causes heart attacks and leads to strokes and all sorts of different health problems. We've also just recently demonstrated that religious involvement is related to immune system functioning." A recent study published in the American Medical Association's *Archives of Internal Medicine* showed that heart patients who had someone praying over them, and here's the amazing part—*even without that person's knowledge*—suffered 10 percent fewer complications than those patients who had no prayers said on their behalf. The whole idea of intercessory prayer, as it's called, has become unbelievably popular within the medical community over the last five years.

But there's another aspect to prayer and healing that's often overlooked. Instead of just focusing on the potential of prayer to help cure the ills of the physical body, many social scientists are noticing that prayer is playing a more prominent role in helping people to decide where, when, and to whom they'll go for medical treatment. Often these decisions are life threatening by themselves. It only makes sense that many people would turn to their faith and God's divine wisdom when confronted with those kinds of choices. Prayer not only helps us heal physically but it guides us through the entire healing process, whatever it may be.

For some, prayer may seem like a roundabout way for the Lord to work. Unfortunately, too often we feel that if we are not immediately healed by prayer, or God doesn't seem to answer, it's because there is something spiritually wrong with us. We feel disheartened and alone, thinking, "Why doesn't God listen to me? Doesn't He understand how badly I need His help?" But as Dr. Billy Graham advises, "We must always submit to the sovereign purpose of God for our lives. God does not always act in the same way in every situation. Sometimes God chooses to heal by a direct miracle. When He does, it is to bring glory and praise to His name; at other times God chooses to heal through natural means and through the knowledge and skill of doctors. We must be careful not to limit God in the way He may choose to heal. We believe He would have us pray for healing and then use any available help such as doctors and medication; at times God may not choose to heal. When He does not, we may be assured that He will provide adequate grace to endure the affliction; when He does not heal, He has a greater purpose in mind. We need to trust our lives completely into His loving care, with the confidence that His ways are always best. Eventually we will understand more clearly what God had in mind in allowing various situations in our lives. But until we see Him face to face, we need to trust fully in His wonderful plan and purpose for us."

With prayer, it's extremely important to keep in mind that it's the process, as much as the end result, that counts. Remember, health is a threefold concept. Even if we are physically feeling under the weather, we become healthier individuals if we tend to the care and nurturing of our minds and souls despite our everyday aches and pains. Ultimately, we will find that we have achieved something extraordinary: a stronger, unified body, mind, and spirit that will allow us to keep laughing, smiling, and happily taking part in the relationships, opportunities, and challenges that shape our lives.

Laughter

Were it not for my little jokes,
I could not bear the burdens of this office.

ABRAHAM LINCOLN

Our final gateway to happiness is Laughter. And I think you'll find that I've saved—if not the best, then at least the most *fun*—for last.

I know you're probably thinking that compared to the other gateways we've already explored, laughter isn't a very serious choice (pun intended!). But as you'll see, that's the point: Each of the other gateways to happiness that we pass through in life—Family, Faith, Relationships, Attitude, Discipline, and Health—involves serious challenges and, invariably, some disappointments along the way. What family, no matter how happy and strong, doesn't have its share of disagreements or conflicts? Whose faith isn't tested by the death of a loved one? Don't we all have days when no matter how hard we try, not only does the glass seem half empty, we even notice that it's a little dirty? Obsessing about those "water spots"—the frustrations, the setbacks, the disappointments—is something that we all do from time to time, no matter how positive our outward attitude or how disciplined we are. And it goes without saying that at some point in our lives, every one of us will inevitably deal with some pretty serious issues involving relationships and health. As we talked about previously, change is one of the few things in life that we can always count on. Sometimes we can see it coming; often we're blindsided by it. But we can't avoid it. All that we have in our power to control is our reaction to it.

And that's why Laughter is the final gateway to happiness. Laughter is like the key we always have under the mat; that secret way we have of opening the door when, for some strange reason, none of our other keys seem to fit. Laughter makes life bearable by helping us to realize that our worries aren't permanent. When we laugh we're able to forget our cares—even if we only forget them for a moment. Every day there are things that make us laugh without warning: a puppy chasing its tail or children giggling and telling each other silly jokes. Children always laugh so easily. Maybe it's time we took a lesson from them. I've always thought that if we really paid attention to how children see the world, they would have more to teach *us* than we could ever teach them.

Even as adults, the pleasure we get from the punch line of a good joke is a pearl beyond price. That's especially true for me. I'm a great audience, but I can *never* remember the punch line when I try to tell a joke myself. Fortunately, when I'm writing it down, I'm more likely to get it right.

There's a good one that I heard recently which pokes fun at how we Texans always like to think *big*. It seems that there's a farmer from Texas who goes to Australia on vacation. While he's there he meets an

Australian farmer and the two become friendly. The Australian invites him back to his ranch to show off his vast expanse of wheat fields. Unimpressed, the Texan says, "Well, they're mighty fine, but we have wheat fields back in Texas that are at least *twice* that big." Then the Australian shows him his herd of cattle. The Texan immediately says, "Well, they're a pretty good size all right, but back in Texas we have longhorns that are at least *twice* as large as your cows." By this point, the Australian is pretty well fed up and the conversation between the two men is at a standstill. Suddenly the Texan sees a herd of kangaroos hopping across a nearby field. Startled, he asks the Australian, "What are *those?!*" Smiling slightly, the Australian replies, "What's the matter, mate, don't you have any *grasshoppers* back in Texas?"

A Laugh a Day Keeps the Doctor Away

How often do *you* really laugh? My motto is to try and have at least one true belly laugh every day. You know the kind I mean. Not a giggle or a chuckle, but the deeper, full-bodied sort of laugh where you think you might actually pull a muscle if you don't stop and catch your breath.

Are you familiar with the scene in the Disney version of *Mary Poppins* where Bert (played by Dick Van Dyke) takes the children to see their kindly old uncle Albert? He serves them a traditional English tea and teaches them to laugh so hard that they, along with the table, chairs, and crumpets, start floating toward the ceiling. *That's* the kind of laughter I mean — laughter so powerful that it lifts you up and away from your everyday cares. Uncle Albert sings a wonderful

He who laughs, lasts.

MARY PETTIBONE
POOLE

song that goes something like, "I love to laugh, loud and long and clear . . . the more I laugh, the more I'm a merrier me." It may sound like a silly children's song, but there's a real message here that we can learn from: Laughter is not only the *result* of merriment; it can *create* merriment and cheer as well.

According to esteemed Dr. James Walsh, people who laugh frequently actually live longer than those who don't. He notes that, "People who laugh actually live longer than those who don't laugh. Few people realize that health actually varies according to the amount of laughter." Back in the sixties, years before Patch Adams began wearing clown noses as a way to help him treat patients, Norman Cousins pioneered the use of laughter to deal with his own life-threatening illness. Cousins, the highly respected publisher of the *Saturday Review*, was diagnosed with ankylosing spondylitis, a severe and extremely painful disease of the spine that affects the joints. In the hospital he was placed on a regimen of anti-inflammatory medications that he felt were as harmful to his body as the disease itself. The drugs, combined with poor hospital food and the fitful sleep that resulted from the requirement that hospitals have to wake a patient regularly during the night to "see how you're doing," made for a treatment protocol that was less than effective. Cousins decided that if he was ever going to get well, he needed to take charge of his own treatment. Instead of the harsh medications, he "prescribed" for himself large amounts of vitamin C and even larger doses of the Marx Brothers and *Candid Camera*. He quickly discovered that, in his words, "ten minutes of genuine belly laughter had an anesthetic effect and would give me at least two hours of painfree sleep." Measuring his progress, Cousins' doctors also witnessed the impact laughter was having on their patient. Immediately following a good laugh, they saw that his inflammation had perceivably decreased. We all owe a debt to Norman Cousins, who, before anyone else, showed us that "laughter is the best medicine."

In the more than thirty years that have now passed since Cousins' breakthrough findings, medical science has advanced to the point where all doctors know that hearty laughter is actually the equivalent of light aerobic exercise. Like prayer or meditation, it boosts our cardiovascular, respiratory, and immune systems by increasing oxygen to the blood and stimulating our muscles. It also relieves stress and tension in the body. But before you get too excited, that doesn't mean watching *I Love Lucy* reruns is a substitute for exercising and eating right. What it *does* mean is that we need to find a way to include humor in every aspect of our daily lives—at work, at home, wherever we go. Laughter is a terrific, inexpensive, and always available tool that we can use to enhance our health and well-being.

You'll probably find this hard to believe, but even *Bela* sometimes used laughter to help us relieve stress and tension before a competition. I'll never forget one incident that transpired at the 1983 American Cup at Madison Square Garden, the competition I described earlier where I was suddenly given the opportunity to compete because one of the girls on the team was injured. Talk about being nervous! I was scared to death. I was going to be competing against some of the biggest names in my sport. The morning of the meet, Bela took me around to all four disciplines: vault, bars, beam, and floor. The warm-ups went extremely well, and even though I knew in my heart that I was ready, I was still petrified. I went into the locker room to change into my competition leotard, and when I came back out, Bela pinned my competition number on my back. He then took his hands, placed them on my shoulders, and turned me around to face him. His always intense green eyes bore straight into mine. I braced myself for his pep talk. And he gave it to me . . . in *Romanian!* He went on for a good two minutes before he saw me start to giggle. He stopped and asked me, in English, "What's so funny Little Body?" Still giggling, I said, "Bela, I didn't understand a single word you just said. I don't *speak*

Romanian." Then he threw his head back and let out that huge bear laugh of his. And with a twinkle in those green eyes, he said, "I'm sorry, Little Body, I forgot." *Sure* he had. And you know what? I'm not exaggerating when I say that the laughter Bela and I shared in those two minutes might very well have made the difference in whether or not I was able to apply all my hours of hard work and training with confidence and ease—and ultimately, between winning and losing. Bela's little joke truly helped to ease my nerves before what was, so far, the most important competition of my life. I won that day, and my victory at the American Cup propelled me closer to earning a spot on the Olympic team.

If we neglect to use humor in dealing with life's problems and challenges we can end up feeling pretty grim—and that can lead to yet another problem: taking ourselves—and our problems—too seriously. Sometimes we actually begin to think of our *problems* as who we are. Just look at some of the terms that people may use to describe us, or worse, that we may use to describe ourselves—words like "divorced" or "unemployed" become long-term statements about who we are, rather than short-term descriptions for issues that we're coping with at a particular point in time. Furthermore, the more we focus on our own crises and frustrations, the less open and available we are to others. Laughter is often the only way we have to keep the more serious and difficult parts of our lives in proper perspective.

Although it may initially seem counterintuitive, laughter is even a good way for some of us to grieve. Just recently, psychologist George Bonanno of Catholic University did a study of bereavement where he videotaped recent widows and widowers talking about their lost spouse. He discovered that those people who laughed one or more times during their recollections seemed much better able to cope with their loss over the long term. Bonanno concluded that not only does laughter help ease the psychological pain of a person who has lost a loved one but that by laughing when we're in mourning, we make it easier for our friends to give us the emotional support we need. So, in the great tradition of the Irish wake, we just might find that laughter can be of help in healing even our deepest wounds.

Smile First, Ask Questions Later

Ella Wilcox, the woman famous for saying "Laugh, and the world laughs with you, weep, and you weep alone" said something else that's always stuck with me: " 'Tis easy enough to be pleasant, when life flows along like a song; But the one worthwhile is the one who will smile when everything goes dead wrong."

Think about how easily you smile when things are going well. You probably smile often without even knowing it. But what about the times when it feels like nothing wonderful is happening in your life whatsoever? We've all had periods where it seems as though we're constantly getting the short end of the stick—we get the flu right before the big party we've been planning to attend for so long; we are passed over for a promotion on the same day our dog is put to sleep; we spend thousands of dollars on a new front porch only to have an off-season hurricane blow through town and wash it away. At times like this, it is very tempting to vent our anger and frustration to the world around us. Some days, nothing seems more appealing than crawling back into bed, burrowing under the covers, and sulking with a big, pouty frown the way we did

True holiness consists of

doing the will of God

with a smile.

MOTHER TERESA

when we were kids. If somebody told you to smile, you'd probably think they were out of their mind.

Turns out, it's not as hard as you think. In fact, it takes more effort *not* to smile. Someone once observed that our faces use twenty-six muscles to smile, but we need *sixty-two* muscles to frown. So smiling is actually a small way to make things easier on yourself. Moreover, if we can get our facial expressions to cooperate, our hearts and minds will often follow. Lifting the corners of your mouth is a first step in lifting your spirits. So the next time you're feeling down, take a deep breath, relax, and try smiling. Although the whole world may not smile with you, I guarantee you'll get a boost.

A few years back I got to have some fun with my reputation as a "smiler" when I did a series of commercials for ESPN, the popular sports television network. In one, I go tumbling through the studio, only stopping long enough to ask a man for directions. He points down a hallway and I just start tumbling off again in that direction. My destination is the SportsCenter booth, where I find one of the anchors and start critiquing his smile. "No," I tell him, "that's not how you do it. That looks phony. Try it *this* way." I keep flashing my smile at him and we can tell he's thinking *"How do I get her away from me?"* That was the whole premise of the campaign, that poor ESPN was plagued by all these athletes who were always hanging around the studio and wouldn't go home. Those commercials were such a blast to shoot! And they turned out to be so popular that a lot of major sports stars agreed to make their way out to small-town Bristol, Connecticut (where ESPN is located), and stay at a Motel 6 just to get to do them. It just goes to show—if you smile a lot, people notice.

I think the funniest spot I did was one that, for some reason, never aired. In it I'm in the SportsCenter control room and, with a completely straight face, I'm trying to convince anchor Robin Roberts that

ESPN should replace its broadcast of NCAA basketball's Final Four with coverage of rhythmic gymnastics. By the end of the commercial I have her cornered and she just looks at me like I'm totally nuts. It was hilarious.

Advertisers know as well as anyone that we all respond positively to things that make us smile. If they can make us laugh through a clever ad campaign, we'll be much more receptive to their sales pitch and more likely to go out and purchase their products. I recommend that you use the same approach when dealing with the people around you. Smiles are infectious, and you'll be amazed at how everyone, including yourself, is positively affected by a warm smile and an upbeat demeanor. Suddenly everything becomes easier—perfect strangers say hello and offer to hold the door for you, the line at the post office seems to move more quickly, and you're not as frustrated when the person in the take-out line at McDonald's gives you a cheeseburger instead of the hamburger you ordered.

Smiling will definitely help you through your day as you're dealing with the outside world, but don't forget that the people closest to you deserve to see your smile too. Sure, you can let your hair down with your family and friends, and that's important. They're there for you whether you're feeling exuberant or just want to be left alone. But don't let that be an excuse for not smiling around the house. As the great poet Maya Angelou says, "If you have only one smile to give, give it to the people you love."

Giving the Gift of Laughter

I've been blessed with a lot of fun jobs in my life, but some of the very best projects I've worked on have involved people whose job it is to make people laugh. I think that giving the gift of laughter—whether you are a professional comedian, a circus performer, or simply enjoy telling a good joke—is one of the noblest vocations around. We've talked about the importance of making laughter a part of our everyday lives, but all too often, it's hard for us to do. That's why these very special people are so necessary: They share their humor and put on performances that shine light into our lives and enable us to find our smile just when we thought we'd lost it forever.

After the Olympics, from time to time a small part in a movie would be offered to me. In 1987, I got a call from someone at Paramount Studios asking if I would be willing to play Tiny Tim in *Scrooged*, a comedy version of *A Christmas Carol*, starring Bill Murray. Would I? You bet I would! I've always been a huge Bill Murray fan, from his first days doing television comedy to his more recent movies. Working with him was an opportunity I couldn't pass up, and I was particularly excited about doing a comic riff on one of my favorite stories, *A Christmas Carol*.

Even though I wasn't an actress, the studio executives assured me that the part didn't really require me to be one. Bill plays a cynical network executive who's casting a sensational television version of *A Christmas Carol* (kind of a movie within a movie) and I was his character's choice to play Tiny Tim. "She won't throw away her crutches," he enthusiastically tells the other executives. "She'll do a double somersault!" All I had to do was learn to tumble while wearing eight layers of clothing and a hat. Piece of cake!

It was such a fantastic experience. I remember walking onto the set for the first time, trying to be inconspicuous, but Bill saw me anyway. He just completely stopped in the middle of a scene and shouted "MAARYY LOOUUU!!!" At first I was mortified—here I was, a complete novice, interrupting the production process and getting in the way of these experienced actors. But he marched right over and gave me a big hug and I couldn't help myself, I just started laughing. Everything Bill does is *so* tremendously funny; humor just radiates from his every move. In fact, he ad-libbed through most of the movie and they used almost all of it in the final cut.

Working with Bill was an absolute dream because his unfaltering sense of humor carried us through the long, grueling hours of filming. And I think that all our hard work paid off. In the end, the film was extremely successful and has become something of a comedy classic. Most important, all of the good-natured humor that Bill shared with us on the set and that was eventually woven into the finished product was brought forth to a larger audience. Hundreds of thousands of people watched and continue to watch that movie—and each time another person laughs or smiles, the world becomes a better place.

As I said before, I'm not an actress and as much fun as acting can be, I really have no desire to become one. Still, this experience was extremely rewarding in that I was able to participate in something that would bring pleasure and laughter to others. Just remember, while we can't all be Bill Murray, we all have it in our power to improve people's lives by finding a way to make them smile or laugh.

Laughter Shouldn't Hurt

I had a teacher in fourth grade, Mrs. Lester, who taught me something that I've never forgotten. "It's fine to laugh, Mary Lou," she used to say, her kind blue eyes focused intently on me, "but remember always to laugh *with* other people, never *at* them." Most of us have heard this aphorism at one time or another, but it's one of those universal rules that will never steer you wrong. I'm teaching this idea to my own

That laughter costs

too much which is

purchased by the

sacrifice of decency.

JOHN QUINTON

daughters already. In fact, I just had an experience with Shayla the other day that illustrates this very distinction. We were in the bank together and she saw a teenage girl with pink and blue spiked hair standing in line ahead of us. She started laughing and pointing at her and I quietly told her that she needed to stop and that it wasn't a nice thing to do. When we got in the car, I explained to her that while most girls don't have pink and blue hair, she shouldn't have laughed at the girl just because she looked different. Shayla, who is very sensitive, was immediately concerned that she might have hurt the teenager's feelings. She said, "Mommy, I hope I didn't make her cry. I don't like it when people are mean to me." I told her that as long as she remembered not to do it the next time she saw someone who looked strange to her, it was okay. But I felt pleased that for just a moment, she was able to put herself in someone else's shoes and feel what it would be like if someone was laughing at *her*.

Who and what we choose to laugh at is an important measure of a person's character. The playwright William Mizner said, "I can usually judge a fellow by what he laughs at." Laughing at something that hurts someone else is never the way to find true happiness. Oh sure, in the short run, you might have a little fun at someone else's expense. But I promise you that in the course of a lifetime you'll find that the more you laugh at other people, the more you'll find that the joke is really on you.

Making the distinction between positive and negative laughter is something that we all need to work on, even as adults. In fact, it's even more important for grown-ups to keep this difference in mind. Children may not understand when or why their behavior is hurtful, but we adults usually know when we are being insensitive—even if we choose to ignore our conscience and join in the humor of the moment. We've all been tempted at one time or another to participate in some of this less-than-appropriate humor. If someone disappoints or offends us, we may try to make ourselves feel better by making fun of their faults or idiosyncrasies. Or perhaps we're standing with a group of friends at a party who are laughing and gossiping about another guest, and we laugh along so we won't appear prudish or feel left out. But I've always believed that, in the same way a warm smile or laugh brings warmth and light into the world, malintentioned laughter envelopes us in a chilly, unpleasant fog.

Malicious jokes and humor may seem like good-natured fun, but the next time you catch yourself making fun of someone else, try to do what Shayla did—put yourself in his or her shoes. Think about how it would feel to be on the receiving end of the jokes and laughter. Chances are you'll find it doesn't feel too good. Laughter is a powerful tool that we can use to dramatically lift the spirits of those around us— but we can dampen those same spirits if we aren't careful. And making someone else feel bad about themselves is never a part of the recipe for happiness. So the next time you're about to have a good laugh at someone else's expense, take a deep breath and change the subject. Better yet, interject something positive about the person and try to diffuse the situation. Remember, hurtful behavior is like a boomerang: In one form or another, it always comes back to you.

Laugh at Yourself

While it's never acceptable to laugh at others, laughing at *yourself* is a different story altogether. Learning to laugh at our own foibles and

You grow up on the day

you have your first real

laugh at yourself.

ETHEL BARRYMORE

lovable personality quirks is one of life's greatest lessons. In doing so, we not only gain a healthier perspective on the complex events that shape our lives—we develop a kind of humility that enables us to interact with the people around us in a more enjoyable and rewarding manner.

After the Olympics in 1984, all the gold medalists went on a gold medal tour around the United States sponsored by the Southland Corporation, which owned all the 7-Elevens in the country. Our first stop was the White House to meet President Ronald Reagan and First Lady Nancy Reagan and present them with commemorative Olympic blazers. The delegation voted on who would present the blazers and Steve Lunquist, who won the gold in swimming, and I were elected. When the big moment came, I marched proudly up to President Reagan, ready to hand him his bright red blazer. At first he just looked down at me (he's actually quite tall, over six feet) in a friendly but sort of neutral way. Then, out of the blue, as though he'd suddenly recognized me, he got this *big* smile on his face and called out across the room—in front of *everybody*—"Nancy, come over here! It's that *little* Mary Lou!"

It's a good thing that a long time before that occasion I'd learn to laugh about references to my size. President Reagan's remark was perfectly innocent and he certainly meant no harm by it. He's a kind, funny, wonderful man and that's how I'll always remember him. Naturally he had no idea that he'd stumbled upon what had one time been something of a sore spot for me. When I was a kid, there were many times when the comments about my height (*"Hey, shorty, what are you going to be for Halloween, a leprechaun?"*) were deliberately cruel and really hurt my feelings. As the baby of my family, I was constantly getting pushed around and picked on by my older siblings. Nevertheless, while being teased about my height when I was growing up wasn't easy, I think it ultimately made me tougher and I *know* it helped me develop a strong sense of humor. Instead of getting angry or upset when kids said something about my being short, I learned to turn it around with a funny remark that showed I had no problem with my height; something like, *"I sure am! I already bought my Lucky Charms!"* Once the other kids saw that I wasn't the slightest bit fazed by their remarks, they lost interest in the joke.

Learning how to laugh at myself was a very important lesson for me. I was never going to be tall, so there was nothing I could do about *that*. The only solution was to figure out how to change the joke so that it wasn't hurtful anymore. Humor and laughter were the methods I found to do just that. Think about it: If you can choose between laughing or crying, which one would you pick?

Self-effacing humor is a sign of humility, which is one of the qualities I most admire in other people and it's something I've always striven to achieve for myself. I once read something by the English writer and critic John Ruskin that has always stuck with me: "The first test of a truly great man is his humility."

As we've discussed, strong self-esteem and a positive self-image are important qualities, no doubt about it. But having *too much* self-esteem can be every bit as unhealthy as having low self-esteem. That's where we run into another real problem—as my mother calls it, "getting a big head." Being overconfident or acting superior toward others is one of the fastest ways to lose the respect and affection of the people around us. Most of us have known someone at one time or another who felt the need to constantly remind us of their achievements, or who managed to fill up an entire conversation talking about their own problems and issues. While we should always strive to get along with others, no matter what their eccentricities, I think it's safe to say that, given the choice, we'd rather spend time with someone else. One of the best ways to keep from taking ourselves too seriously and alienating those around us is to learn how and when to laugh at ourselves. I'm not talking about making yourself into a clown or a buffoon. There's absolutely a difference between putting yourself down in earnestness and engaging in a little self-deprecatory humor.

The thing about laughing at yourself is that it completely disarms anybody who's trying to embarrass you. If you can genuinely laugh about your own perceived shortcomings, then you automatically take the power away from anyone who might try to make you feel insecure. As Elsa Maxwell, the grand hostess renowned for her sparkling dinner parties once advised, "Laugh at yourself first, before anyone else can."

There have been countless times when having a sense of humor about myself has made a potentially awkward or uncomfortable situation much easier to deal with. Oddly enough, two most memorable occasions both involved autograph seekers.

During the '96 Summer Games in Atlanta, I participated at a big promotional event at the Marriott Marquis hotel. After it ended, I tried to make a quick escape, but the van I was supposed to ride in was blocked by traffic and couldn't pull away from the front of the hotel. The lobby was packed with people leaving the dinner, many of whom recognized me, and the crowd was beginning to descend on me all at once. It was total chaos and believe it or not, I started to get a little nervous. I usually don't mind giving autographs, but when hundreds of people with pens are rushing toward you, it's definitely time to run for cover!

Thanks to a kind bellman, I managed to escape to a baggage storage room near the front desk, where I was able to wait out the crowd safely. You should have seen the startled looks on the faces of folks who came in looking for their luggage. Instead of their suitcases, they found me sitting cross-legged on the counter, handing out baggage tags and having a great time just laughing at the whole situation.

Now, I know plenty of celebrities—or even regular folks—who would have been absolutely outraged if they had been trapped in a baggage storage room, hiding from noisy crowds and unable to get home to their families. But rather than allowing myself to get all stressed out about the situation, I chose to see the humor in what was happening to me. I wasn't at all embarrassed to be handing out luggage tickets rather than signing autographs for fans—I was getting a huge kick out of chatting with the surprised hotel guests and wondering amusedly, "How did I end up back here?"

The other story is a perfect example of how people can quite unintentionally and easily take you down a peg if you're starting to get a big head. I was in a grocery store not long ago and a woman came up to me in the produce section shrieking and carrying on about how she was so excited to meet me. I was a bit taken aback, but my fans mean a lot to me and I wanted to give her the autograph she asked for. And of course, I was flattered by all the attention. She didn't have any paper on her so she actually went through the line with just a banana, bought it, and came back for me to sign the peel! But as strange as that was, the peel wasn't even the best part of the story. When she looked at the banana, her face just fell and she wore a look of utter disappointment. "Oh," she said, "I thought you were Dorothy Hamill."

Boy, that kind of thing can bring you back to earth in a hurry! Another person might have been offended, but when I got home, Shannon and I were doubled over in hysterics laughing about it. In fact, he called me "Dorothy" for a week. Rather than be upset by the woman's mistake, I chose to simply see the incident for what it was: a gentle, extremely humorous reminder that, to most of the world, Mary

Lou Retton is just another name in the phone book. And of course, it was a wonderfully amusing story that I frequently share with others, and that inevitably incites more than a few chuckles.

But my favorite story by far about the benefits of being able to take the kidding of others in good spirits involves the time that I first met Michael Jordan. If I hadn't had a sense of humor, we might never have become friends; I would have been way too intimidated by him. During the 1984 Olympics in Los Angeles, the U.S. Olympic Committee had no choice but to split the various teams up into two communities on account of our size. Half of us stayed on the USC campus, and the rest were housed at UCLA. You would have thought they would have put the gymnastics team at UCLA because that's where we were competing, but they didn't—we were bunking at USC. So on the day of the opening ceremonies at the Coliseum, as we were walking out of the dorms at USC, the volunteers instructed us to board any of the numerous buses that were waiting there on the street. Purely by chance, I climbed onto the same bus that was transporting the entire U.S. Men's Basketball Team.

Even back then, I certainly knew who Michael Jordan was. Growing up with three brothers, there was no way I could not know about him and his unbelievable success at North Carolina. So I was suitably impressed and delighted at the prospect of having a chance to talk to him. I didn't have much time to be in awe, however, because the teasing began the moment I stepped on the bus. "Hey, there's a height limit to board this bus," Jordan called out. Patrick Ewing yelled, "Are you as tall as Charlie Brown?" (referring to those cut-out characters you have to measure yourself against in order to get on the rides at an amusement park).

The humor in the situation wasn't lost on me. It truly was a funny sight. Here you had the tallest athletes at the Games and me, quite literally one of the smallest, all together on the same bus. It was great! I loved it. My ego wasn't bruised at all—it was like having your big brothers picking on you, and I've certainly had plenty of experience with that. It was probably one of the funniest bus rides I've ever had. The big guys were cracking jokes and singing their favorite tunes, and I loved it that I was able to laugh it off and get in the spirit of the situation. Of course, when we arrived at the Coliseum for the opening ceremonies, there was media *everywhere*. And they insisted on taking my photo with Patrick Ewing, who at seven feet was the tallest athlete competing in the Games. The picture in the paper the next day looked like something taken at a circus sideshow!

Then, we all hugged good-bye (okay, they patted me on the head and I hugged their *knees*) and wished each other good luck. Years later, Michael and I joked about that ride when we were together at an event for Wheaties. And, true to form, he was still making wisecracks about my height even there. So, the minute he wasn't looking, I took a spoonful of Wheaties (which I was supposed to feed him for the cameras) and shoved it right in his mouth. We both laughed until our sides hurt.

The point is, none of that—the great media moment when we stepped off the bus; the exchange of support among fellow athletes; and best of all, my friendship with Michael—would have been possible if, from that very first moment when I boarded that bus, I hadn't smiled right back at all those somewhat intimidating giants and said, "You're right, there *is* a height limit on this bus—and you guys are all *over* the limit. Now everybody off!" Laughing at yourself, and getting others to laugh with you, is one of the best ways we have of growing closer to people.

Laughter Breeds Togetherness

Someone once said that if you get people laughing, you know they're listening and you can tell them almost anything. I've certainly found that to be true when I'm giving my motivational speeches to seminars and corporate groups around the country. Not only do I play off my height in my opening remarks in order to better engage my audience, I also point out that if they learn to view laughter as a valuable tool in their professional lives, they can use it to increase their own effectiveness in whatever business they happen to be in. Of course, I'm not just talking about telling jokes around the water cooler. Used properly, laughter can help decrease stressful situations in the workplace, which, in turn, can become a major factor in increasing worker satisfaction and productivity. It helps create a feeling of camaraderie among employees, and brings more of that warmth and light we talked about into the office environment.

It might sound corny, but when we make someone laugh, we're actually giving them love. As far as I'm concerned, laughter is one of the strongest bonds that I can have with another person, and that includes my husband and my children. In fact, one of the main reasons I fell in love with Shannon was because of his crazy sense of humor. He always knew just how to make me laugh, whether I was stressed beyond belief with final exams in college, or about to give birth to our first child. And, after fifteen years together, he still does.

Shannon actually proposed to me in the funniest, most original way I've ever heard about. I'd been away giving a speech, and he came to pick me up at the airport. Driving back into town, we had to pass through a toll booth on the highway. When we pulled up alongside the booth, instead of letting us through, the attendant suddenly came out and started to approach my side of the car. Now I have a rather fertile imagination, and a number of scenarios—none of them good—popped into my mind to explain his actions. Needless to say, I was more than a little nervous. But I kept my composure, and tried to convince myself that he was probably just a fan who wanted an autograph. Then, when he got to my window, instead of handing me a pen, he handed me an envelope with my *name* on it! Looking worriedly at Shannon, who was trying hard to keep a blank expression on his face, I took the envelope and opened it. The note inside read, "Mary Lou, I love you. Will you marry me?" I turned back to Shannon, who was now grinning from ear to ear (as was the toll booth attendant), and he handed me a small box with a ring inside. I started laughing and crying at the same time, pummeling him on the shoulder for scaring me and hugging him for making me so happy. We still laugh about how scared I was, but it was the most hilarious, most romantic moment of my entire life. Even though we were laughing rather than kissing, I knew right then with absolute certainty that the love between us had never been stronger and that he was the soul mate God intended me to spend my life with.

We're all practical jokers in our family, and the laughter that ensues is a key part of what holds us together. There's one good story that just happened recently, but before I tell it, you need to understand something about Shannon. In a real crisis, he's the bravest, strongest person I know. He's my rock, and I cherish the support he gives me in every way. But the silliest little things can spook him. For example, if he walks into a dark room and I'm hiding somewhere waiting to surprise him, even if he *knows* I'm in there, he still jumps.

Now I've been known to pull this sort of stunt quite often during our fifteen years together. His reactions are so perfect that I just can't resist. So, just the other day, I took one of our daughters' toys—a small, gray, stuffed mouse that looks extremely realistic—and hatched a plan. We'd been swimming all morning with the girls and I came inside to prepare lunch for everyone while Shannon stayed in the pool with Shayla and McKenna. Shortly after, I called them all inside for lunch. I'd placed the mouse on the kitchen floor right by the back door so that the minute he walked in, he would have to see it. Knowing exactly what would happen, I couldn't stop giggling. Just when the door opened, I screamed in my best frightened little girl voice, "Oh my word, a mouse!" You should have seen Shannon. And *heard* him. He jumped up so high I thought his head would hit the ceiling. At this point, I was practically on the floor, I was crying so hard with laughter. When he finally realized what had happened, he chased me around the island in our kitchen, caught me, and wrestled me back down to the floor where he could tickle me. To tickle me is to torture me. We were both laughing so hard that we could barely catch our breath. At that moment, our daughters came into the house, and saw us both on the floor laughing hysterically, so they did the only sensible thing. They ran over, jumped on our pile, and joined in.

It's those amazing moments, when your voices ring forth with peels of laughter and your sides hurt and you look at each other and start giggling all over again, that you know you are sharing an incredibly intimate experience, and that for one moment you are truly and deeply connected with the other people around you. Laughter is the final gateway to happiness because it unites us with others and with God in an inimitable, spontaneous, and deeply fulfilling manner. That's what I mean when I say to you that the gift of laughter is truly the gift of love.

SO AS YOU CONTINUE on your own journey toward happiness, I leave you with this final bit of wisdom: When you stumble upon one of life's many roadblocks, and especially when the road is smooth, laugh. Laugh every day. Laugh loud enough so the Lord can hear it. Let your laughter be the heartfelt expression of the happiness that you find as you cross through the seventh gateway and continue down your chosen path to an extraordinary life of love, accomplishment, contentment, and peace. I wish you every success along the way.